Praise for 33 Ways Not to Screw up Your Business Podcast

I've been podcasting for over a decade, and still learned some new things from Alastair's book.
It's clear, concise, and pragmatic - perfect for anyone new to podcasting.
If you're serious about starting your first business podcast, I guarantee that reading *"33 Ways Not to Screw up Your Business Podcast"* will be well worth your time and money.

— **Jonathan Stark**, author of "*Hourly Billing Is Nuts*", host of the "*Ditching Hourly*" podcast and "*The Business of Authority*" podcast

If you are a card carrying POD-crastinator, this book is for you!

> Alastair has assembled a fool proof plan to help you get up and running with your business podcast.
> After podcasting for over 7 years (800 plus episodes!) I've discovered multiple ways to screw up my podcast!
> Alastair is going to help you avoid many of the newbie mistakes that we all fall victim to.

— **Adam Schaeuble**, podcasting coach, and host of *Podcasting Business School*

> Bloody LOVE it!
> A great book that cuts to the chase and delivers a distilled version of what anyone with podcasting dreams needs to know.
> The highlighted importance of getting clear on what you want your podcast to do for your business is insightful.

— **Gill Moakes**, podcaster, business coach & growth strategist

> This is the first book I've read that really treats podcasting as a business and not a hobby. If you're looking to build a good

> revenue stream from your podcast, you need this book.

— **Joe Casabona**, podcasting coach, and host of *How I Built It*

> Alastair has put together a truly comprehensive resource for the podcast rookie — without being overwhelming!

— **Judson Rollins**, consultant, and host of *Propel Your Revenue*

33 Ways Not to Screw up Your Business Podcast

A comprehensive guide to planning, recording and launching your business podcast

Alastair McDermott

Best of luck with your show!

Alastair

Networlding Publishing Inc.

For more information or for bulk sales, contact support@therecognizedauthority.com

ISBN 9781955750530 (Paperback)

ISBN 9781955750547 (Ebook)

ISBN 9781955750554 (Audiobook)

Published by Networlding Publishing Inc., Chicago, Illinois.

This book is part of the 33 Ways Not to Screw Up series of short, actionable business books from Networlding Publishing.

This edition: v1.06 last updated 7th Feb 2023

Disclaimer

Additional Resources

Acccess a complete and regularly updated list of links, resources, tools, and websites recommended in this book, including:

- your free podcast launch workbook from the author
- recommended podcast equipment list, including links and reviews of audio & video equipment
- links to example Guest FAQ pages
- links to example Media Kit pages
- links to third party resources including the State of Business Podcasting Report, and more

You can access the online resources page here: **rec.nz/resources**

Contents

Foreword

If you're building an expertise business, you've probably wrestled with the question: to podcast or not to podcast?

It's a little too easy to dismiss podcasting out of hand: "I hate the sound of my own voice", "Where will I find the time?" "Who will edit the darned thing?" "How will I get interesting guests?"

But as Alastair McDermott makes abundantly clear, there are work-arounds to all of these, plus the dozens of other excuses and fears rolling around in your head.

Instead, look at it this way: podcasting is — hands down — the quickest road to authority when you approach it strategically. When you align it with not only your business goals but your personal talents and passions. When you set yourself up for success.

That means designing a podcast that will position you firmly in the minds of your ideal clients and buyers as an expert, an authority-in-the-making. As an emerging voice in the niche you've decided to claim for yourself.

That means having your podcast play a distinct role in how you monetize your expertise — because that authority you're building will lead you to services, products and price tags you're only fantasizing about now.

And, it means using your podcast as another way to "sell" your expertise — not with traditional sales techniques but because your listeners have come to know, like and respect you. You've warmed them up so they actually want to buy from you — without ever asking for the sale.

Sounds like a tall order, doesn't it?

That's why I'm such a fan of Alastair's approach to successful podcasting: it breaks it down into small, easily executable steps. It takes the mystery out of podcasting and puts you firmly in control of your destiny as an authority.

I first met Alastair when I guested on his podcast The Recognized Authority. We clicked immediately since we share many of the same beliefs about building authority in the expertise space.

And, he's an unflappable host — which he demonstrated the second time I guested with a giant steamroller grinding and beeping outside my window (I'm still in awe of how he managed to salvage that recording).

So naturally, I was happy to read 33 Ways Not

To Screw Up Your Business Podcast. And happier still when I saw how perfectly he oriented this book to new podcasters ready to tackle building their authority in public.

Once this book is in your hands, you'll not only read the whole thing, you'll be ready to immediately put the lessons into action for your business.

Read it fast — then read it again and take notes. Then buy a copy for everyone you know who is procrastinating on starting their business podcast.

Rochelle Moulton

Author of *The Authority Code: How to Position, Monetize and Sell Your Expertise*

California, October 2022

Introduction

I wrote this book because I'm passionate about helping business owners like you to share your expertise and advice.

Why? One of the most valuable long-term investments you can make in your business is to build your authority and credibility.

> **"Is there a benefit to sharing your work, in teaching other people? If you don't share, write, and produce content how else will people discover you?"**
> — Chris Do, Emmy award-winning designer & founder of The Futur speaking on *The Recognized Authority* Episode 69

There is only one route to authority: **demonstrating your expertise in public in some way.**

Traditionally, that meant you had to write a book,

and find a publisher willing to print it. But more recently we've seen blogging, video, and podcasting spring up as viable — and possibly even superior — alternatives.

All of these formats and channels have their pros and cons for you, the creator, and for your audience who consume your content.

As a channel, podcasting has some major differences built-in that make it advantageous for us, notably speed, consistency, engagement, and relationships.

Speed: it's one of the quickest ways to start creating content. You could start planning your podcast today, and realistically have your first episode live in 24-48 hours. I wouldn't recommend rushing it to that extent, but it could be done.

Even if it takes you weeks to prepare, record, and launch your podcast, that still compares favorably with other options like writing a book.

It's also much quicker to create the actual content. If I asked you to write 800 to 1,000 words about a topic, how long would that take? If I put a microphone in front of you and asked you to tell me about it instead, that 1,000 words would take you about 5 minutes to speak.

Consistency: most podcasts have a regular release schedule. That means your audience engages with your thinking on a consistent basis, and many will even make your podcast part of their weekly routine.

From your perspective as a creator, the regular release schedule allows you to create a routine too — allowing you to build a workflow that fits into your schedule.

Engagement: podcasts allow your audience to consume your thinking without having to look at a screen. They can listen while doing other things, like driving, exercising, gardening, or doing chores. Your podcast is not competing for attention with fifty open browser tabs.

Relationships: I'll give you the backstory to the creation of this book to demonstrate.

I have a podcast — of course — called *The Recognized Authority*. Last year, I interviewed Anne Janzer, an author, and after the interview we chatted in the post-show. Anne said "You should interview my publisher, Melissa Wilson, she'd be a fantastic guest!"

And so I reached out to Melissa and invited her on the show, and she was a fantastic guest. After the interview, we chatted in the post-show — you're seeing the pattern here, right? — and she said "Alastair, would you be interested in writing a book for the *33 Ways* series?"

I'm honored to have Rochelle Moulton, author of *The Authority Code*, write the foreword for this book. At this point you won't be shocked to learn that Rochelle was a guest not once, but twice on *The Recognized Authority*.

I met Rochelle through Jonathan Stark, who is a business coach I've worked with to help with my business. Jonathan was also the first guest I had on my podcast, and after the interview we chatted in the post-show and I asked him if he could introduce me to Rochelle so I could invite her on the podcast.

That's the other huge advantage of podcasting — it allows you to build relationships with great people.

You can leverage your show to speak with people you wouldn't have access to otherwise. For example, I've spoken with Alan Weiss, Carol Cox, Chris Do, Monique Mills, and Marcus Sheridan. They are all renowned authorities in their fields, and it's having the platform of my podcast that allowed me to speak with them, and build these relationships.

Podcasting is incredibly valuable, but it can also be tricky to get started.

There's a hundred different decisions to make, some minor with minimal impact, and others major strategic decisions that can determine your success or failure.

I've written this book to help you navigate those decisions, and to help you avoid making the mistakes I've made myself, and seen others make.

Let's get started!

PART 1: Designing Your Podcast

1: Have a clear goal

Most podcasts fail, and fail quickly. The quickest way to "podfade" is to start without clear business goals.

Starting and sustaining a podcast is a lot of work, and having clear goals will guide you as you make decisions.

The good news is having a podcast can help you achieve several different business goals — some compatible with others, some less so.

Start with the end in mind

Follow Steven Covey's advice "start with the end in mind" and you'll start off on the right foot. Think about what you want to achieve with your podcast.

If you're an independent business owner like me, you might want to establish your authority and personal brand, demonstrate your expertise, and build relationships with clients.

If you work in a larger firm, you might want to use the podcast to help recruit employees.

Podcast goals

Your goals could include:

- Growing your audience
- Establishing you as an authority & thought leader
- Building relationships with potential clients
- Building relationships with authorities in your field
- Recruiting great employees
- Monetization through sales of your services or products
- Monetization through sponsorship

Every decision you make around the podcast should be framed in the context of achieving those goals, from naming the podcast to the format you choose to how long the episodes are.

One way to think about this is where your ideal clients fit in your podcast.

For a podcast focusing primarily on business development, your guests might be your ideal clients. For a podcast focusing primarily on building authority, your listeners might be your ideal clients, and your guests are industry experts.

Reality usually isn't quite as clear-cut. Podcasts are great for achieving multiple goals at the same time, so you might have significant overlap.

That's okay, it's your podcast, and you make the rules!

2: Target a specific audience

The most important aspect of podcast planning is to pick a clear, specific target audience.

Not for everyone

Don't try to create a podcast for "everyone". Those podcasts end up being bland, lacking personality, and find it impossible to stand out.

Instead, start with a specific target audience. For example, if you're in the fitness space, rather than targeting the entire weight-loss category you might choose "people who want to lose weight through VR gaming", or "women who want to start back running after having a baby".

If you're in marketing, rather than targeting all businesses, target a niche like "hotel furniture manufacturers", "mid-size cargo transport operators", or "men's fashion ecommerce stores".

By the way, those are all real examples of actual businesses, and while not all of them have podcasts yet, I think they would be interesting enough for their target audience to listen to.

Niching down is counter-intuitive

It seems counter-intuitive, but the more you niche down, the better. You're moving from competing in the ocean to competing in a much smaller pond.

- You will stand out from the crowd.
- Your podcast will be more appealing to listeners in the niche audience.
- Your content will naturally be more interesting as you're forced to make it relevant for your audience.

If you're not sure where to start with picking a niche, check out *The Specialization Podcast* at **SpecializationPodcast.com**

3: Choose a topic you love talking about

This should be obvious, but surprisingly some podcasters don't love the topic they're talking about, and it shows!

It's a mistake to pick a topic purely based on popularity. When you love the topic you're talking about, your passion shows through in your voice and energy. Your listeners will pick up and appreciate it.

It makes it a whole lot easier to sustain a podcast for months and years when you love the topic.

You don't need to be an expert, yet

The good news is you don't need to be an expert on the topic when you start! If you spend months or years podcasting about a topic, talking to experts in the field, your knowledge will inevitably grow over time. Interviewing experts is a fantastic way to learn, as is researching and planning solo episodes.

If the topic niche seems overcrowded, you might want to niche down further to a subtopic with less competition, but it's a positive sign if there are already several podcasts covering the topic.

Competition means the topic has been validated to some degree, and your fellow podcasters make for great guests for your podcast and might even reciprocate by having you guest on their show too!

One other thing to bear in mind is that you will naturally expand and diversify what you cover over time, exploring related topics. That diversification is good if there's a clear link between topics and your listeners have an interest in them. I would suggest focusing on the core topic first, then branching out later after you've developed your style and built an audience.

It's okay to tweak things

You can also tweak and adjust the topic over time — it's your podcast, and you can do what you want with it! For example, after 20 episodes, I renamed my interview show from *Marketing for Consultants* to *The Recognized Authority*. Even though the name changed, I still cover exactly the same topics, just with more focused branding.

Obviously, it would be better not to make drastic changes that might confuse or irritate your listeners, but it's absolutely fine to make changes that are congruent with your topic, your business, and your goals.

Whatever topic you choose, talking about something that you have a genuine passion for will help you stay motivated and avoid burnout.

4: Pick a format that lets you start easily

When you're creating a podcast you've got a lot of choices to make. One of the most interesting choices is the format of the podcast — do you want to have an interview show, a solo show, or a show with a regular co-host? This decision comes back to your podcast goal: what you want to achieve with the podcast.

Here's a rundown of options you can choose from, and who they might be a good fit for, starting with the more popular traditional format options

Interview podcast

The classic interview show is the most popular format, where you interview a different guest on each episode of your podcast.

The content is naturally baked into the conversational format, you can do as much — or as little — preparation as you'd like.

The interview show comes with a network effect:

you can reach new audiences if your guests share the episode with their social networks — that isn't guaranteed to happen, but you can help by making it easy for them to share — see elsewhere in this book for more on that.

You can choose who to bring onto your interview show — it's a great way to build relationships with people you couldn't normally access. That could be well-known authorities in your field, or you could bring on guests that you've identified as potential clients of your business.

The downside of an interview podcast is that you are putting the guest on a pedestal to showcase their expertise. It can be difficult to showcase your own expertise and build your authority in that context.

Co-host podcast

Co-host podcasts are "buddy shows" where the same co-hosts take part in each episode. These often make for very popular podcasts when the co-hosts have a great rapport and have fun. Some podcasts have a panel of co-hosts and rotate in and out each episode, and I don't think it's a coincidence that my favorite podcasts to listen to are in the co-host format, including *2Bobs* with David C. Baker and Blair Enns, and *The Business of Authority* with Rochelle Moulton and Jonathan Stark.

This format can work really well if the co-hosts already have a large audience, but bear in mind that you won't get the same network effect as interviewing a different guest each week — unless you want to bring a guest into it too! It's your podcast, you get to choose.

Solo podcast

The solo format is where you pull up a mic and start recording yourself. This is the simplest of all podcast formats, but also one of the toughest to pull off.

Solo podcasts can foster a more intimate connection with your listener as you are talking directly to them. But you need to be careful not to bore them as you don't have the change-up of voice that comes with another person on the audio. You can help break up the monotony of the monolog by varying your tone of voice, the speed that you speak, and even introducing breaks with audio "stings" like you hear on the radio.

For solo episodes, it's important to outline your podcast in advance and open with an attention-grabbing hook that opens a loop in their head.

Evergreen, educational podcast

One format that is hugely interesting is an evergreen, educational podcast. I first saw this from Seth Godin, where he recorded a 2-day workshop for entrepreneurs called *Startup School.*

Seth published it as a 15-episode evergreen podcast in 2012, and it's been online for over a decade, helping entrepreneurs, building his authority, and acting as a top-of-funnel device.

You can listen to *Spotlight Podcasting's* Jonathan Baillie Strong and I discussing the benefits of the evergreen podcast format in Episode 65 of *The Recognized Authority*, available at rec.nz/65

Coaching podcast

You could record coaching sessions with clients — only with permission, of course — to show what it's like working with you. I've done this on *The Recognized Authority*, Natalie Eckdahl does this on her *Bizchix* podcast, and Jonathan Stark does this on *Ditching Hourly.*

Hybrid show

You can pick a hybrid format, where you have a mix of different formats in different episodes of your podcast, or even different formats within a single episode.

Repurpose other content

You can repurpose other content to your podcast, e.g. **YouTube videos,** recordings of **conference talks, webinars**, or even **panel discussions**.

You can use this repurposed content to supplement your regular podcast episodes, and in fact, mixing it up can help keep listeners engaged.

What I picked for my podcasts

I chose **interview show** as the primary format for *The Recognized Authority* because I wanted to create a sustainable, long-term audience-building podcast. However, to help build my own authority and credibility, I occasionally publish solo episodes and — with permission — republish my appearances on other people's podcasts.

I chose the **evergreen, educational model** for *The Specialization Podcast*, in order to quickly create an asset that generates leads for my business and positions me as an authority on specialization. It was far quicker for me to record this podcast than to write a book, and it works in a similar fashion in building authority.

I again chose **interview show** as the format for *Accelerating Your Authority* because I wanted to interview my ideal clients in a short form, higher-frequency podcast than *The Recognized Authority*. Having a separate podcast for this allowed me to optimize the workflow to automate more, and turn around publishing episodes more efficiently.

It's your show and your choice! Just remember that whatever you choose to do, you need to keep it sustainable over the long term.

5: Pick a short name

Naming your new podcast is an important step in creating your podcast.

It's important because it sets the tone for what your show is all about and helps you stand out in the sea of podcasts.

It is a significant decision and so I have some specific tips to help you.

But before we get to that, I want to reassure you of something: the podcast name is not set in stone.

You can change the name later

I've renamed my podcast, as have plenty of other podcasters. I changed mine from *Marketing for Consultants* to *The Recognized Authority* after 20 episodes. In fact, if you go back and listen, you can hear the different introduction.

Obviously it's better to pick something fantastic and stick with it, but don't let the naming decision bog down your progress. Choose something good enough, and get moving!

My tips for choosing a podcast name

Here are some tips to guide you through the process.

1. Keep it short and sweet: Aim for a name that is 4 words or less, and memorable so that listeners will be more likely to recommend your podcast to others..

2. Avoid using your personal name: Unless you have established a personal brand and large audience, it's best to choose a name that is in line with your topic rather than using your own name.

3. Relevance is key: Your name should reflect the content and theme of your podcast.

4. Branding: Your podcast name should reflect the tone and style of your show. If your show is humorous, your name should reflect that. If your show is serious and informative, your name should reflect that as well.

5. Zoom out a level: Choose your topic and then move up one level of abstraction up, so that your name has room to grow as your show evolves. This also means that if you want to

bring guests on, they will feel like they can contribute to the discussion.

6. Say it out loud: Practice saying your potential names out loud to see how they sound.
7. Availability: Make sure the name is available as a domain name and is not in use for another podcast - search Apple Podcasts and Spotify.
8. Test the name: Before finalizing your podcast name, try it out on a few friends, family members, and potential listeners. Get their feedback and see if they think the name accurately represents your show.
9. Avoid common words: Don't include the word "the" or "podcast" in your title, and try to choose a name that is unique and sets your show apart from others.
10. Consider search: Think about how your name will appear in search engines and, if possible, include keywords related to your niche.

In conclusion, choose a name that accurately represents the content and style of your show, is memorable, relevant, and unique.

And remember, if you don't love the name, you can always change it later. The most important thing is to start creating and sharing your content!

6: Pick a frequency you can stick to

Podcasting is a long-term play. You need to show up consistently.

Consistency builds trust. Publishing regularly over a significant period of time demonstrates to your audience that you are reliable and in it for the long term.

Listeners will start to bring your podcast into their routine once they trust that you will show up at the same time, every time. That allows them to develop a "parasocial" relationship with you, where they feel like they know and trust you.

I release *The Recognized Authority* at 6:01 am every Monday and have done so for over 100 episodes. I've gotten emails from listeners in several different countries telling me how it's part of their Monday morning routine.

Workflow

There are a lot of moving parts involved in releasing

a podcast episode. Some of that will depend on your choice of format, and whether you create individual episode cover art, but at a very minimum you'll be recording and editing audio, writing show notes for each episode, and uploading it to your podcast host.

You need good workflows to produce a podcast episode time after time. Ideally, you'll delegate as much of the heavy lifting as possible, leaving you free to concentrate on producing great content.

Release frequency

When you're considering frequency, there are acceleration effects to consider: the more often you release, the quicker you'll build an audience and see benefits for your business. On the other hand, you risk burning out if it's more frequent than you can handle.

Daily

You risk burning out, but it can and has been done by many podcasters, led by John Lee Dumas and his *Entrepreneurs on Fire* podcast which has over 2,000 episodes at this point! If you can keep up with a daily show your learning curve will be very quick and you should see acceleration effects coming into play where you grow faster than your less frequently published peers.

You can do weekdays only to give yourself a bit of space, and use batching to record a week's worth of episodes in an afternoon. Alternatively, you could record on a live stream — see the section on formats for more on that subject.

Weekly

The most common release schedule for active podcasts is weekly. It's a sweet spot for a lot of podcasters. With a weekly release, your regular listeners can make your podcast part of their routine. If your podcast is 20-45 minutes, you're probably spending 2-3 hours a week recording and on production.

Monthly & quarterly

I know some podcasters who release at a slower pace like monthly or quarterly. It's less likely that it will become part of your listener's routine, but it still has some value in positioning you as an authority and demonstrating your expertise.

One-off

I mentioned an evergreen, educational podcast series in the format discussion. I think there's a place for these one-off podcast series, and that's underscored by the fact that Seth Godin's *Startup School* podcast is still live and hasn't been updated in a decade.

7: Do a fixed-length first season

Rather than launching your podcast with an open-ended goal, you can plan to do a fixed-length first season.

A podcast season is similar to a TV show, it separates the episodes into self-contained blocks.

Seasons give you a natural break

Having seasons gives you a number of advantages. It's a natural break that gives you a chance to step back and evaluate how the podcast is working for you.

It's an opportunity to vary the show theme between seasons — this is particularly useful for educational podcasts. You could change up the format, from solo to interview or bring in a new co-host. You could even switch up the publishing schedule, although I'd be wary of changing the schedule too much as you might lose regular listeners.

The break gives you a rest. It means you get a chance to step off the publishing treadmill, you can take time to recharge and get excited about the next season.

You choose the season length

With seasons, you choose what works best for you, from the number of episodes in a season to the frequency of publishing to the length of break between seasons.

It's entirely up to you how you do it. Take a cue from TV where even shows with similar formats can have entirely different approaches to season length. Take *CSI: Miami* which regularly had 24-25 episodes per season, and the BBC's *Sherlock* which took a very different approach with only 3 episodes per season.

Short first season is great for testing

If you're completely new to podcasting, you might want to commit to a first season of 8-12 episodes. That will give you an early break to implement feedback, pivot, change workflow, release schedule or even change the podcast format.

Longer season builds momentum

If you're a regular podcast listener and have been

planning for a long time, you might plan for the first season of 50 or even 100 episodes. That's what I did with *The Recognized Authority*, taking a short hiatus at Episode 100 to evaluate the format and options

Seek listener feedback

One thing you can do with seasons is to ask for feedback from your listeners as you're coming to the end of the season. Create a short survey asking them what they love about the show and what doesn't work so well for them. You can ask them about the topics, the frequency, the episode length and the format. Use the feedback to plan your next season to make it even better.

Tell listeners what they can expect

The final piece of advice with seasons is to tell your listeners about it! Tell them when you're planning to take a break and when you'll be back. They're far more likely to stick around if they know what's going on.

8: Listen to other podcasts

I've interviewed a lot of successful podcasters, and there are certain patterns that jump out. The most noticeable thing is that all the best podcasters I've spoken to are avid podcast listeners.

You can learn a great deal from listening to other podcasts that you can then apply to your own show. That includes how other formats work, what length show you like listening to, new or better questions you could ask your guests, to how long your intro segment could be and what it could include.

Listeners create shows that are listener-focused

When you're planning your own show as a regular podcast listener, you have a much better idea what will work for your listeners. You know what you love and hate as a podcast listener, so you can incorporate or drop those elements from your show.

Get familiar with your niche & peers

You can discover your peers' podcasts and get to know their style and particular angles on your topic. You can figure out who you want to bring onto your podcast as a guest, because you know they'll probably reciprocate. And you'll know who you want to steer well clear of because of a clash of values.

Find great guests

By listening to other podcasts, quite often you'll come across people who are fantastic guests, and you'll want to have them on your show too. You even have a built-in reason to connect with them, telling them you heard them on the other show, or you could even ask the host to introduce you to difficult to reach high-profile guests.

9: Create distinctive cover artwork

Along with your podcast name, your cover art is one of the first things a potential listener will see. They'll see it in the middle of a list of other podcasts, so it needs to stand out.

Communicate the subject of the podcast

The number one job of the podcast artwork is to show potential listeners what the podcast is about. It should be instantly recognizable to people who are already familiar with your brand.

Congruent branding

That means using the same color scheme and fonts that you do for your business logo & brand visuals. Using these similar visuals will help your clients recognize your podcast when they see it in their podcast app or scrolling through social media.

Big and small

When you're designing the artwork, you should create it as a large image file — 3,000 pixels by 3,000 pixels — as that's the size Apple prefers.

But bear in mind that it will be displayed in many different places in various sizes, and in fact it will most commonly be displayed as a small thumbnail image in podcast apps, directories, and search results.

Large title text

That's why I recommend keeping the text simple, and have the podcast title as the primary text on the cover. Don't crowd the image - there's not enough space to include your tagline, and while you can include the host name, I'd keep it small.

Simple images

It's acceptable to go with a text-only cover, particularly if you're using visually interesting colors & fonts. If you use an image, what you choose gives potential listeners a message about the topic & style of the podcast. Here are my recommendations for the image choice.

- Don't use a photo of the host unless you're a

celebrity or very well-known in your field.

- Don't use a "podcast" image like a microphone, headphones, pop-filters, etc.
- Use a photo or illustration that is representative of the topic in some way.

Compare with other podcast covers

Check out other podcasts in your niche and have a look at their cover artwork. If your podcast was listed alongside them, would it stand out?

Here are some online tools where you can preview your cover art alongside other podcasts, and even how it will look in the podcast apps.

- transistor.fm/preview
- onlypod.com/podcast-cover-preview

You can change it later

Don't worry if it's not perfect at the start, as your cover is something that you can change later. It is important, so do the best you can. But don't let trying to create the perfect cover get in the way of launching your podcast!

PART 2: Setting Up Your Podcast

10: Get the right equipment

When you're starting out podcasting, you need to tread a careful line.

You can't allow a lack of knowledge or equipment to prevent you from getting started. At the same time, there is a minimum level of audio quality that you should be aiming for.

That's why you'll often see contradictory advice given to podcast newbies: "don't worry at all about podcast audio quality" or "audio is crucial, so you should buy the best equipment".

The truth is somewhere in between. You *can* use a phone headset, or AirPods, or a built-in laptop microphone. But there's a huge quality difference between those options and a standalone microphone, even at the entry-level end of the market.

Dynamic range vs condenser microphones

There are two major categories of microphone you can choose from:

1. dynamic range microphones

2. condenser microphones

I recommend you use a dynamic range microphone.

This is somewhat controversial, because condenser microphones are more sensitive.

But a more sensitive microphone isn't always "better", and a condenser microphone will often pick up traffic noise, the hum of a computer fan, or a dog barking several blocks away, while a dynamic microphone recording in the same environment will only record your voice.

Dynamic microphones are less sensitive and don't tend to pick up very quiet sounds.

In my experience that tends to be more important in a business environment where you don't have a sound-proof recording studio.

USB vs XLR microphone

The other major consideration in what microphone to choose is the connection type, and again there are two major options:

1. XLR

2. USB

I recommend USB.

XLR is the studio standard for professional audio created in the 1940s and used by musicians worldwide.

XLR microphones require an audio interface — another piece of equipment — to convert the analog XLR signal to a digital audio signal that your computer can understand.

USB microphones will plug directly into any desktop or laptop computer without any extra equipment, and that's why I recommend you start with a USB microphone.

Audio equipment recommendations

I think most business podcasters should invest at least $50 to $100 in a microphone. That's not a huge amount of money for an important piece of equipment.

If you're looking for a simple recommendations, these are the microphones I recommend at various price points

- The *Logitech H390* is a $40 USB headset that is good enough to get you started without spending a lot of money.

- The *ATR2100X* and the *Samson Q2U* are both fantastic $80 to $100 microphones used by many podcasters.

- The $250 *Shure MV7* will give you studio-quality audio while still having the convenience of USB that plugs into any desktop or laptop computer. This is my number one recommendation to anyone starting a podcast for the first time.

Yes, there are higher end options like the popular *Shure SM7B*, *Rode Procaster*, *ElectroVoice RE320* or more expensive *RE20*, and a host of other broadcast quality microphones.

These are all XLR microphones so you'll *also* need to purchase an audio interface, and depending on the mic, a preamplifier or booster too. The investment for this kind of setup starts around $600 and you can easily spend four or five times that.

Boom arm

Apart from the microphone, you might also want to invest in a suspension boom arm to hold the microphone in a convenient position. This allows you to position the microphone close to your mouth without you having to lean forward, or have a tripod block access to your keyboard. It also can reduce vibrations and shock noises from your keyboard and table.

I started out with a cheap suspension arm that worked for years, and recently upgraded it to a more expensive professional boom arm. The advantage of the more expensive boom arm over their cheaper counterparts is they're usually more robust, have a longer reach, can hold a heavier microphone with ease, and are quieter to adjust.

My audio setup

Here's my audio setup now, and a few notes on what I used previously.

1. **Microphone**: I started out with the *ATR2100* which I used for about ten years, and recently upgraded to the *Shure SM7B*.

2. **Boom Arm**: I now have a *Gator Frameworks* boom arm, after using a cheap suspension arm from eBay for years.

3. **Audio Interface**: I use an *Audient Evo 4* audio interface to connect the microphone to my computer.

4. **Gain Booster**: Because the *SM7B* needs a gain boost, I use a *Triton Audio Fethead*.

Note that I only need the audio interface (3) and gain booster (4) because of my microphone choice.

If I had gone with a USB microphone — e.g. the *Shure MV7* like I recommend you — I'd have saved some money, desk space, and some technical headaches in setting it all up!

I have some videos showing some of the equipment I've mentioned here, including the *Logitech H390* headset, the *ATR2100*, the *Shure SM7B*. You can find that linked on the resources page for the book at **rec.nz/resources**

11: Create a good recording environment

I know I've already mentioned the importance of podcast audio quality but bear with me if reiterate: audio quality is crucial.

If your podcast sounds like it was recorded over a bad phone line by someone sitting in an empty bathtub, that will cost you listeners.

Reverberation, or reverb, is an aspect of sound quality that is 100% in your control. Reverb is the audio engineer's term for echo, it sounds terrible in podcasts, and makes speech more difficult for the listener's brain to process.

Reverb occurs when you create sound — usually with your voice. Those soundwaves go out in all directions, travelling the short distance directly to the microphone, and also travelling longer distances until they meet a surface, like a wall, window or floor.

In an acoustically-treated recording studio, those travelling soundwaves are captured and don't reflect back. But in an untreated bare-walled office, they do bounce back, arriving fractions of a second later at the microphone, causing reverb.

It's virtually impossible to remove it in the edit, so you should aim to reduce reverb in your recording space as much as possible. The good news is that reducing reverb can be quite simple.

Cover hard, flat surfaces

Look for hard, flat surfaces in your recording space and cover them with something soft and uneven. A legitimate way to kill reverb is to fill your room with "stuff" — soft furniture, rugs, and full bookshelves are all great at diffusing & absorbing sound waves. Pull curtains closed over windows. Cover floors with rugs — this is your excuse to get a deep-pile rug for your office! Break up large bare walls with acoustic panels, book-cases, or even blankets.

My friend, Megan Dougherty, describes this wonderfully as "recreating your teenage bedroom" with clothes strewn everywhere — that's *perfect* for recording podcasts.

Acoustic panels

Acoustic panels are sections of sound-absorbing materials, and are highly-effective at controlling reverb. They also look fantastic!

They come in all shapes, sizes, colors, and

materials, from the standard inexpensive black foam "egg-box" tiles you've probably seen on TV, to expensive 3D wooden diffusers that are de facto works of art.

Acoustic panels are very often used as video backdrop as apart from promoting great sound, they also make for a great looking background.

Position your acoustic panels on the places on the wall where sound waves tend to hit first. That's around 4 to 5 feet (1.2 to 1.5 metres) from the ground, which is the typical height of a person sitting down. The most important wall to cover is the one facing directly towards you, but also cover the walls to your left and right, and behind you if you have enough panels.

Get closer to the mic

When you watch singers and people on stage, notice how they work to make sure they're always speaking close to the microphone. You *dramatically* improve your audio quality by simply getting your mouth close to the microphone.

A good rule of thumb is to have one fist-length of distance between your mouth and the microphone. For most of us that's around 3-4 inches (7-9cm)!

12: Record video too

Podcasts are traditionally audio-first productions, but that's changing rapidly, and if at all possible, I strongly encourage you to record video of your solo episodes and guest interviews.

The future is video

Video has become a major factor in podcast production. YouTube has added podcasts to their top level categories, and video is still growing rapidly in social media - just take a look at the war for attention between TikTok and Instagram.

Creating authority-building content

Creating content for social media is at the same time probably the single most *important* thing you can do to build your authority & credibility, and probably the single most *time-consuming* thing you can do to grow your business.

Recording a video podcast allows you to create

an abundance of great authority-building video in a time-efficient manner.

There are two main types of video that you can create with your podcast.

1. Publishing your full episode as a video.
2. Publishing short clips from the episode.

With YouTube now actively promoting podcasts, I recommend publishing your full episode videos there, either to a new channel dedicated to the podcast, or to a dedicated playlist on your existing channel.

Identifying and pulling out short clips from your episodes can be time-consuming but also hugely beneficial to growing your podcast. Find 30-90 second clips where you or your guest share an important point, and post these on social media as a teaser for the episode. Make sure to have captions enabled as up to 92% *[NextTV]* of social media viewers watch without sound!

Video adds complexity

When you add video to the mix, it does add complexity. You need to consider your background, lighting, and camera angle. You might want to upgrade your camera. Your editing workflow will probably change, and outsourcing video editing is more expensive than outsourcing audio editing.

Video takes practice

There's a learning curve that comes with recording video. The good news is that practice will pay off quickly, but you need to start. Your first videos may not be Oscar winning productions, but just like going to the gym, the more reps you put in, the easier it will become, and you'll be producing great videos after a few weeks or months.

Audio is the highest priority

Audio is always the highest priority, even if you're producing a video for YouTube or other social media. Viewers will sit through a video with poor picture quality and great audio, but they won't tolerate poor audio quality even if you have amazing 4K Ultra HD picture quality.

Fill the frame

If you're talking on video, you should be filling the picture frame on-screen. The top of your head should be just below where the camera cuts off. Avoid the unflattering "up the nostril" shot that laptops often give you — stack some books underneath to raise it so you get as close to straight-on as possible.

Look at the camera

This is one of the hardest things to train yourself to do, but makes a massive difference to the viewer: look right down the barrel of the camera lens as often as you can.

When you look directly into the camera it feels like direct eye contact to viewers. This is particularly important when you know that there will be an audience watching the video either live or afterwards.

It is difficult, and you will need to practice. Most people look down at their screen where the other person is appearing. It's okay to do this every so often, but try to spend as much time as you can looking directly at the camera.

Lighting is crucial

A cheap $30 desk lamp can do more to improve your video quality than a $1,000 camera. You need to make sure you are facing the light, so it's shining on your face, rather than having it behind you, e.g. sitting with your back to a window. Your lights should not be directly on camera. Ambient, indirect lighting is softer and avoids harsh shadows, which is usually our preference in business video.

If you want to upgrade your lighting setup, go with a traditional three-point lighting setup.

1. The primary light is the *key-light* shining on you from the front, at an angle.

2. The *fill-light* is from the front on the other side from the key-light.

3. The *back-light* is behind you.

I recommend checking out dimmable LED lights like the *Elgato Key Light* series.

Video equipment recommendations

If you want to produce good video, start with a decent webcam. The $140 *Razer Kiyo Pro*, $200 *Elgato Facecam* or $200 *Logitech Brio* are top of the range webcams. The *Razer* comes with a built in ring light, which is great if you don't have good lighting.

The next step up is mirrorless or DSLR camera, and brings a new level of picture quality but also complexity. I recommend the $700 *Sony ZV 1* "vlogging" mirrorless camera, or the $750 *Sony A6100* with the $400 *Sigma 16mm F1.4* lens if you have a higher budget and want to get a blurred background effect.

Advanced tip: A blurred background with the subject in focus in the foreground is a visually appealing look achieved by having a shallow depth-of-field. It is known as a "bokeh" effect.

You need additional hardware to connect a regular camera to your computer as a webcam. I recommend the *Elgato Cam Link 4K*.

If you're using a mirrorless or DSLR camera as a webcam, I strongly recommend you get a "dummy battery" — this is an empty battery shell for your camera that has a wire coming out from the bottom that connects directly to a power source like a USB or wall socket.

This allows long-term, continuous operation of your camera, removing the need to swap out your camera battery on a regular basis. It also avoids battery heat being generated inside the camera. Double- and triple-check that you get the right one for your camera, and note the voltage that it requires.

My video setup

I use the *Sony A6100* camera with a *Sigma 16mm F1.4* lens, plugged into *Elgato Cam Link 4K,* with a *Neewer DC Coupler Replacement for NP-FW50 Dummy Battery Power Adapter with USB Cable.*

For lighting, I use four dimmable *Phillips Hue* lights as fill-lights and back-lights. These give soft, indirect ambient lighting that removes most shadows. I also have two dimmable LED lights to either side, which serve as a key-light.

More resources on audio & video

If you want more tips on audio/video equipment and setup, I've written a book to help you with that. Published by Oak Tree Press, it's called *How to Sound & Look Good on Zoom & Podcasts*

You can get a free copy by visiting the online resources page here: **rec.nz/resources**

13: Choose reliable podcast hosting

Your podcast host is where your podcast audio files are stored. Podcast hosts all provide similar functionality — when you are ready to publish an episode, you upload it to your host and hit the publish button.

There are a ton of options, and just like I recommend for website hosting, I recommend that you pick a provider who is going to be around for a long time.

I have two strong recommendations for what not to do with podcast hosting.

Do not host your podcast audio files on your own website

Unless you are a server technology expert, I strongly recommend you do not host your podcast files yourself on your own website.

That's because your website hosting is almost certainly not set up to store and serve large volumes of audio files that have spikes in download behavior as new episodes are released.

Do not use free podcast hosting

I recommend you don't use free hosting, based on the adage "if it's free, you are the product" — this is particularly true for a business podcast where your podcast impacts your brand.

Podcast hosting is relatively inexpensive and should be worth investing $20-50/month.

Choosing a host

Here are some considerations when you're choosing your podcast hosting company.

1. Are they going to be around in 5 years time? Moving hosts is possible but it is definitely a hassle.

2. What storage limitations do they have? This might involve some math. For example, The Recognized Authority publishes around 60 episodes of average 45 minutes each per year. That's approximately 1.5GB of storage.

3. What bandwidth limitations do they have? This is often counted by number of downloads, and depends on the size of

your audience. A successful business podcast might have 5-10,000 downloads per episode. If you are starting from scratch, getting to 500 downloads per episode can be hard work.

4. Do you have complete ownership & control of your podcast? This is particularly important to check if you are using a free or very low-cost service.

5. Do they support the major podcast directories? They should support Apple Podcasts, Google Podcasts, Spotify and more. Check the list of supported directories before you sign up.

Podcast hosting companies

Larger podcast hosting companies include *Acast, Anchor*, *Blubrry*, *Buzzsprout*, *Podbean*, and *Spreaker*.

These six hosts have gone through an extensive certification process to have their analytics vetted by the *Interactive Advertising Bureau* (IAB). This isn't a direct reflection of their quality as a podcast hosting provider, but I think it speaks to their commitment to the long-term and so I'm listing them first.

Other major podcast hosts include *bCast*, *Captivate*, *Castos*, *Fireside*, *Resonate*, *RSS.com*, *Simplecast*, and *Transistor*. These are all well known and recommended by many podcasters.

There are hundreds of smaller podcast hosting companies. In fact there's too many for me to list here, but I will keep a list of recommendations I get from other podcasters in the online resources page here: **rec.nz/resources**

PART 3: Launching Your Podcast

14: Publish a trailer in advance of launch

Give your audience a sneak preview of your podcast by creating a trailer.

Just like trailers for movies & TV shows, a podcast trailer helps build anticipation and lets your audience know what they'll be getting when the podcast launches.

A podcast trailer introduces your show and your host(s) to the audience. It explains what it's going to be about and teases some of the topics. You can share some audio clips — highlights from episodes you've already recorded.

Pique their interest

Build some curiosity and tension by leaving some questions unanswered. And just like a regular podcast episode, you should give the listener a clear next step — tell them how to subscribe, and when the episodes will be coming.

Your trailer can be as short as 60 seconds, or as

long as 15 minutes — it's entirely up to you. You can publish the audio version to your podcast feed as an "Episode Zero" — all good podcast hosts support tagging an episode as a trailer.

If you create the trailer as a video, you can also share it to YouTube and the other social networks — that will help build your audience more.

Your trailer helps test your setup

Publishing a podcast trailer to your podcast feed in advance of the main podcast launch date has an additional benefit — it helps you test your podcast feeds and make sure everything is working as it should.

It's quite normal for podcast directories like Apple Podcasts to take a few days or even several weeks before your podcast becomes available. Getting that set up before launch with a trailer helps you test that everything is working as it should.

15: Launch with several episodes

When you're launching your podcast, I recommend you don't launch too early. Wait until you have several episodes produced and ready to publish together as a batch.

Here's what I recommend:

1. Publish your podcast trailer a week or two before launch.
2. Publish 3-5 episodes on launch day.
3. Have another 3-5 episodes ready to go — this is your safety buffer.

Let them binge

You give listeners who find your podcast a chance to binge on multiple episodes, rather than finding just a single episode and having to wait for more.

The fact that there are several episodes also shows them you're committed to the podcast, and are worth their time and attention.

Demonstrate your range

When you publish several episodes, you can also address multiple topics and show the listener what the podcast is going to cover in the future.

It increases your "surface area of luck" by providing more opportunities for your audience to discover and share your content.

You simply have more episodes to market and promote during your launch! If you have only one episode, your promotion can get boring very quickly.

16: List your podcast everywhere

You put a significant amount of time and money into creating your podcast. From recording and editing to show notes and cover art, it's a lot of work. So you'll want to share it with the world. Do just that.

Podcast RSS Feed

Every podcast has a podcast "RSS feed". This is an address to a file that contains all the information about your podcast & episodes in a machine-readable format. When you submit to directories and apps, they read that information to learn all the details of your podcast. They will then periodically check your RSS feed to check for new episodes.

For example, the podcast RSS feed for *The Specialization Podcast* looks like this: **https://feed.pod.co/the-specialization-podcast** — just like mine, your feed will probably include your podcast host name and the podcast name.

Submit your podcast feed to all the major podcast apps and directories. By doing that, you'll ensure that it shows up when potential listeners search within their favorite podcast app. There's also a search engine optimization benefit for your website if you're linking to it in your podcast — which you should be — see the section on this elsewhere in this book.

Apple Podcasts

You want to make sure that your podcast RSS feed is submitted to *Apple Podcasts* — the major player in the podcast world — and also to the other podcast apps and directories.

Most good podcast hosting companies will have built-in tools to help submit your feed to some of these directories and apps, but you'll need to submit some of them manually too.

Every directory is different. Some of them will require that you create a free account before submitting your feed, and some won't.

List of directories

I suggest that you get your podcast listed on *Apple Podcasts, Spotify, Google Podcasts, Amazon Music,* and *Audible*, and as many of the rest of these as you can: *Podcast Index, TuneIn Radio, Stitcher, Pandora, iHeart Radio, Listen Notes, Castbox, Miro, PocketCasts, Podknife, Podchaser, Samsung Podcasts, Deezer, Player.FM*, and *Plazoo*.

There are more, and this list will change over time, so have a look to see what options are available, and put an annual reminder in your calendar to add it to new directories that appear on the scene. You can find an up-to-date list of directories on the online resources page here: **rec.nz/resources**

PART 4: Fine-tuning Your Podcast

17: Write great episode titles

Episode titles are normally the deciding factor for someone listening to your episode or not.

They're a significant factor in listeners subscribing to your podcast and helping new listeners find your podcast through search.

Think about someone looking at your podcast in their smartphone podcast app. What do they see? The podcast name, maybe a short description, a small thumbnail with the artwork, and often they'll see the list of episode titles.

One podcast I saw titled every podcast episode with a format like this: "Episode 12: A Conversation with John Smith".

The problem is their episode listing in Apple Podcasts and podcast players looks like this:

- Ep 24: A Conversation w...
- Ep 23: A Conversation w...
- Ep 22: A Conversation w...

This is off-putting for potential listeners as they have no idea what the episodes are about without further investigation. And it will kill your discoverability in search.

Instead, lead with what the episode is about — specifically address the main topics of conversation.

Use copywriting headline templates to construct more interesting headlines — remember that the purpose of the episode title is to entice readers to listen to the episode. Answer the question "Why should I spend time listening to this?"

Episode Title "Do's and Don'ts"

Here are some rules of thumb you can follow to help get your titles right.

Start with the topic

The first words a potential listener will see are crucial, so tell them what it's about. What will they learn or discover if they listen to the episode? Try to clearly communicate the topic of the episode.

Be succinct

Podcasts are typically listened to on smartphones, other mobile devices, and even in-car systems. There's not a lot of screen space to display episode titles so use it wisely. The average episode title is 23-27 characters — that's around 5 to 7 words. Personally I make them a little bit longer, usually

40-60 characters, around 6 to 10 words.

Be consistent

Every episode title should be unique but use a consistent format for your titles to make them easily read in podcast apps.

Include your guest's name

Whether to add guest names in episode titles vs the episode author field has been a topic of discussion in the podcast world. On the Apple Podcast for Creators "Present your podcast" page they specifically mention including guest names in the episode title, and so my take on this is to add the name here. I simply put "with Guest Name" after the main topic or title of the episode. If your guests tend to be very well-known you could include the guest name at the start of the episode title, but I'd recommend putting the topic first as that's usually what the listener will care about most.

Don't be clever

It's very tempting to use inside jokes or other clever titles, but that will get you far less exposure and search traffic than simply saying what the podcast is about.

Don't include the podcast name

It's simply not necessary to include the podcast name (in full or abbreviated) in the episode title, as it will appear elsewhere every time the episode is listed. Adding the podcast name uses up valuable space. The exception for this rule is if you have a "meta" episode of some kind, i.e. an episode about the podcast itself, for example, the podcast trailer or a behind the scenes episode — in those rare cases, including the podcast name seems natural.

Don't include the episode number

Podcast apps will list your episode number alongside the podcast episode title, so there's no need to include the episode number in the title itself. Your listeners won't be all that interested in the episode number either, what they care about is whether that particular episode will entertain or educate them on the topic. Apple has also told us that they don't want episode numbers in the title.

Don't include the date

The publish date is already included by all good podcast hosts, so don't waste space with this. The only exception might be for daily news-based shows, but do more investigation if you're going to do this.

Don't use the words "podcast" or "episode"

The listener is looking at your podcast episode in a podcast app or listing, they don't need to be told it's an episode of your podcast.

Don't use "keyword stuffing"

Keyword-stuffing is when you include a large number of keywords into podcast episode titles, descriptions, etc. This is done to try to game the search algorithms, but it's a terrible idea and a great way to get your podcast kicked out of Apple Podcasts.

Example podcast episode titles

Here are some examples of podcast episodes from my own podcasts and some popular podcasts on Apple Podcasts.

The "how to" title

I really like these because everyone loves learning how to do something. This is also the format used by John Lee Dumas of Entrepreneurs on Fire.

- How to Scale Your Consulting Business with Brad Farris
- How to Build Your Personal Brand with Mark Schaefer
- How to Be a Key Person of Influence with Chris Do

The "warning" or "mistake"

Humans are naturally motivated more by moving away from negatives than towards positives.

- Don't Overthink Your Content with Teodora Pirciu
- Sell Expertise, Not Your Hands with Kevin C. Whelan

- You Don't Need to Be Unique to Stand Out with Belinda Weaver

Straightforward statement of topic

You can simply state what the episode is about. This is similar to the "how to" title, but more succinct and better if the topic part needs more description.

- Earning and Holding Attention with Ian Brodie
- The Compound Effect of Content with A. Lee Judge
- Building Your Audience with Dan Sanchez

Ask a question

You can create an "open loop" by asking a question as the episode title. I don't use this one much with guest episodes, but I think it's a great fit for solo episodes. Here's a few examples I found of this on Apple Podcasts:

- Is your learning culture keeping pace with rapid digitalization?
- Real Estate Investing Vs. Stocks: Which Is Better Right Now?
- Can the gig-economy help hotel housekeeping?: Assaf Karmon, TurnoverBNB

Episode titles from popular podcasts

I've taken a random selection of these from a variety of podcasts that Apple is ranking in the top 50 Business podcasts, and I have only included the episode title verbatim so if the podcast name is included, that's how they wrote the title.

Notice the length, how the episode number feels irrelevant here, and how the longest title gets cut off "The Journe..."

- How inequality helps make the business cycle such a beast (Planet Money+)
- From Dreaming to Doing: How We Set and Achieve Goals
- Tunde Oyeneyin On How to SPEAK with Purpose
- Crypto 101: blockchains, currencies and security
- Wisdom Wednesday: 3 Clarifying Questions For A Profitable Lead Magnet
- 388 | The 18-Year-Old Who Actually Listened
- Creating Retirement Security with James Conole
- Spencer Jakab on the Death of Meme Stocks
- #143 Andrew Wilkinson: Entrepreneurial

Insights

- 345: Life is All Based On The Decisions That YOU Make. So Live a Good One.
- #613: Russ Roberts on Lessons from F.A. Hayek and Nassim Taleb, Decision-Making Insights from Charles Darwin, The Dangers of Scientism, Wild Problems in Life and the Decisions That Define Us, Learnings from the Talmud, The Role of Prayer, and The Journe

Mix it up

My final suggestion for your episode titles is to keep each episode title unique, so that when listeners scroll through your list of episodes they see an interesting mix of content, rather than the same thing every time. The exception is if you're doing a mini-series of episodes on the same topic!

18: Create an opening hook

Attention is currency.

The movie *Fight Club* starts with a man tied to a chair with a gun in his face, and the camera cuts to a van full of explosives in the parking lot. It comes back to the protagonist who tells us "it all begins with a girl called Marla" ... cue flashback, and we're into the backstory.

We're not supposed to talk about *Fight Club*, so I can't tell you any more.

CSI Miami starts each episode with a crime being committed, and Horatio delivering a cheesy pun while putting on his sunglasses.

The first episode of TV series *Breaking Bad* opens to an RV careening wildly along a desert track. We're shown that the driver is only wearing underwear, and a gas-mask, and we can hear sirens in the distance.

Netflix' series *Stranger Things* starts with a scientist in a lab coat dashing madly down a dark corridor as alarms ring in the background and warning lights flash. There's a shadow moving behind him.

With your podcast, you may not be making a TV series or movie, but the same principle applies: grab the listener's attention as soon as possible, ideally right from the start.

Open a loop in their brain

That open loop creates tension, a reason for them to continue listening. They have to find out more so that they can close the loop. This works in TV, in movies, in books, even in social media posts. It also works in podcast episodes.

Why should I care about this?

Right at the start of the episode is when they're deciding whether to listen to the full episode or not. It might be a returning listener, or it might be their first time listening to your podcast, and even more important to get them to listen to more of the episode. They are asking themselves a single question: "Why should I care about this?"

Attention is currency, and the opening hook buys you some time.

After the cold open, that's a good time to play your opening sequence, a call to action, or deliver some background information.

If you have an interview show, a simple way to create an opening hook is to have a "cold open" at the start of each episode where you play an interesting clip from the guest speaking later in the conversation.

For solo shows you can open a loop yourself by asking a question or bringing up something interesting or intriguing and telling the listener you'll come back to this.

For my interview podcast, the timeline looks like this:

1. Cold open: a 5-15 second quote from my guest speaking
2. Voiceover intro with music for ~12 seconds
3. A short call to action talking about my coaching offer around ~20 seconds
4. Then I introduce today's guest and start the conversation

Two tips for picking a good guest quote:

1. Choose a quote from their 3rd, 4th or 5th answer, once they've warmed up a bit and are explaining something interesting
2. Ask the same question on every episode, and use their answer to that question as the cold open. For example, I ask "What's your

> number one tip for anyone who wants to build their authority?" and the answer always makes for a good cold open.

The goal is to get them to listen to the episode. Get creative with your opening hook — take inspiration from other podcasts, TV, movies and even books!

19: Include a call to action in every episode

A call to action (CTA) is a clear "next step" you can offer your listeners.

Each piece of content you create can — and should — have a call to action at the end, giving a clear next step for the audience to take.

That includes people listening to your podcast episodes, interacting with your website, your blog posts, your social media posts, and even listening to you guesting on other podcasts.

The call to action is crucially important because it is the connecting glue between people consuming your content, and taking action to become your subscribers and clients.

Offer a single, clear call to action each time

It is difficult to resist the temptation to offer multiple options, but all that will do is confuse the listener and make it harder for them to remember what to do next. Don't complicate things — in each podcast episode offer the listener a single action to take as the next step.

The next logical step

Your call to action is going to depend on your show's goals. In all likelihood you have multiple goals for the podcast, and so you need to choose just one of those goals to focus on in each episode.

You may decide the most important thing for you is to get people to your website to opt-in for some kind of free gift so that you can get them on your email list.

Alternatively, growing your podcast might be the most important thing for you right now, and so you might choose to ask them to rate & review your podcast in their favorite podcast app.

The perfect call to action

Here are some rules of thumb to creating the perfect call to action for your podcast.

1. **Keep it short.** Your call to action doesn't have to be long and complicated — in fact, making it short and sweet will get you better results.

2. **Start with a specific, action verb.** "Download", "listen", "review", "share".

3. **State a clear benefit.** Tell them why they should take action, and how they'll benefit from doing so.

4. **Make it easy to take action.** The listener is driving, or at the gym, or doing household chores. They probably have their phone podcast app open, but their hands are full. In that context, how can you make it easier for them to take action? One thing you can do is use simpler, more memorable website addresses. Or even better, tell them that the web address is listed in the shownotes, so all they have to do is open that in their podcast app.

5. **Deliver with enthusiasm.** One of the benefits of the podcast medium is the listener hears your voice, so add some enthusiasm when you read the call to action.

Call to action examples

Here's a number of real-life call to action examples from actual podcasts covering different goals and contexts.

Rate and review

"Please consider taking 60-seconds to leave an honest review and rating for the podcast on Apple Podcasts,

they're extremely helpful when it comes to the ranking of the show and you can bet that I read every single one of them personally!"

Visit the episode webpage

"Come to the blog post for this episode at TheBingeFactor.com, where you will be able to find and connect to everything Alastair McDermott works on!"

Email subscription and schedule call

"Download your free investment guide and schedule your call today."

This is technically a two-part call to action, but there's a clear relationship between the two pieces.

Email subscription

"Real quick before we get started, I just want to make sure you are subscribed to my newsletter Build Something Weekly. Every week I send a free email to everyone's inbox with insights on what's going on in WordPress and podcasting, you get a rundown of all of the content I created, and you get a summary and top takeaways from this episode.

So if you check your inbox on Monday mornings, and you're like, yes, this is an episode I definitely want to listen to right now, you can. If you're like, oh, wait, a little bit later, you can do that too. You can sign up for Build Something Weekly over at buildsomething.email. That's buildsomething.email for my free weekly newsletter."

Promoting your podcast when guesting elsewhere

"If your listeners would like to hear more about this topic, look for my podcast The Recognized Authority in your podcast app, just search for The Recognized Authority in the podcast search! I particularly recommend you check out my conversation with Chris Do, that's episode number 69."

20: Choose the right guests

If you go with an interview show, then you have an important decision to make around who you bring on the podcast as your guest.

Speaking with interview guests is my favorite part of podcasting. It's the payoff for all the hard work put into the planning, production, and promotion process.

But there are some mistakes to avoid.

Consider your podcast goals

When deciding who to bring on to interview, think about how having those guests will serve the overall goal of your post.

Interviewing your peers & high-profile names in your niche can help you build credibility and your audience. Interviewing your ideal clients is a great way to build relationships and start a conversation. Interviewing people from outside your niche can bring an interesting new perspective to your audience.

Don't expect too much from featuring high-profile guests

Many podcasters start out wanting to have high-profile guests on their podcast. These can feel like the answer to growing your podcast by introducing it to a large, new audience as well as giving you credibility and authority.

The truth is that high-profile guests do help your credibility and authority by association. They're giving it implicit approval just by appearing on your show, saying "I trust this person enough to appear on their podcast". (That's why you should be careful which shows you appear on).

But they don't always bring the spike in audience growth that podcasters might expect. In fact, high-profile guests very often do less promotion of their appearance on your show than lower-profile guests do.

Use guests to get high-profile guests

It's still worth getting them, because the credibility and authority by association is hugely valuable.

It's difficult to get them right at the start, as high-profile people tend to be very busy, and unless you have a prior relationship, it's unlikely they'll agree to come on an unknown podcast with a handful of episodes and fewer listeners.

But later, especially if you've featured some guests that they recognize, they'll be more likely to agree.

Real-life example

I wanted to invite Chris Do on *The Recognized Authority*, but I had no personal relationship with him. Chris is a very busy guy with millions of followers. How could I get him to agree to come on the show?

Here's what I tweeted him:

> @theChrisDo What do you NOT have in common with Alan Weiss, Ron Baker, Jonathan Stark, David C. Baker & Marcus Sheridan?
> You haven't been on my podcast yet!
> Hit me up, I'd love to get you on to chat about all things building authority.
> 10:37 PM · Apr 19, 2022 · Twitter

Just 45 minutes after I sent this, I got a DM from Chris with his booking link.

He appeared on the show four weeks later — check out **rec.nz/69** to listen to that episode.

Why did this work so effectively? I knew for certain that Chris knows all of those people I name-checked, because he's either mentioned their books in his content, been a guest on their podcasts, or had them come to guest on his own podcast.

Start with existing relationships

But how did I get those other people on? I started with existing relationships.

- I've worked with a number of business coaches who have helped me with my business, including Jonathan Stark and Philip Morgan. Both of those instantly agreed to be on the show even before it launched (episodes 2 and 7, respectively).

- David C. Baker doesn't guest on a lot of podcasts and at the start of our call he told me that the only reason he even considered it was because Philip had been on.

- Mark Schaefer came on because of a pre-existing relationship. I had attended his *The Uprising Summit*, plus I'm sure having the previous guests didn't hurt.

- Ron Baker came on because I had Jonathan, David and Mark, and I know Ron was on Jonathan's podcast talking about pricing.

- I knew that Alan Weiss would make for a great guest, as he's kind of a spiky character — in fact I asked him directly about that and you can hear his answer on episode 62 (rec.nz/62). I knew that Alan had written a book about Value Based Pricing, and it's impossible to do that without knowing of Ron Baker, so I'm sure seeing his name helped.

As you can see, there's a compounding effect here where it becomes easier over time as you get higher profile guests on.

You need to be in it for the long-haul, this is not a short-term game. Identify high-profile guests you'd like to have come on the show. Follow them on their social networks, subscribe to their emails, listen to their podcasts, and learn who they respect & follow. Start to engage with those people too. Make it a long-term habit.

Finding guests

I know that finding guests is difficult for some folks. I've never found it all that difficult. Here's how I found the 100+ guests I've spoken with so far.

First, I made a list of experts I know in areas related to the podcast topic. This list had about 25 names on it when I started, and I knew I wouldn't get all of them immediately.

I looked for podcasts that covered the same topics, and made a list of all of their hosts. This is an important category of guest because there's a good chance that they'll reciprocate the invitation and have me on their show.

Those two things got me to about fifty names, which is a year's worth of guests if you're doing a weekly show.

I now get most of my guests from social media, usually *LinkedIn*, but it doesn't have to just be online — I've even found an interesting guest on a *Netflix* documentary!

When someone says something that I find insightful, I look at their profile to see if they'd make for an interesting guest for my audience. If they are, I send them an invite — detailed below.

I also ask my existing guests in the post-interview chat if they have suggestions for who I should have on the show, and for a warm introduction if possible.

I also ask for guest suggestions from my followers on social media, and from my email list.

What makes the "right" guest

I think the choice of guest is part of the personality of a podcast. I can't tell you what would make someone the right guest for your podcast, but I can share what I look for in a guest.

1. Their topic or story must be relevant to my audience. It doesn't have to be *obviously* relevant, and in fact I enjoy finding guests from outside the traditional circles, but it does have to be relevant in some way.

2. They know their stuff. This is a judgment call I make based on what they've posted to social media, and I'm okay with bringing on guests who are still traveling on their journey to authority or success or whatever their goal is.

3. They show some personality. This doesn't mean they have to be a controversial or polarizing person, but having a point of view, some character, that adds some depth to the conversation.

4. They are not overly self-promotional. I find that the more competent they are, the less likely they are to be overtly self-promotional. In fact, I have not had a guest on *The Recognized Authority* who has pitched me — I like to find them myself!

5. I avoid red flags. I don't want to give a platform to people with business practices or views that I find unethical or unsavory. That's

typically "get rich quick", internet-marketing types. If they have a Lamborghini or private jet on their marketing materials, that's not someone I want to promote!

The "Greatest Connection Message"

Inviting someone to be on your podcast is probably the greatest LinkedIn connection request you can send. It's putting them on a pedestal, inviting them in front of your audience.

I usually send potential guests a connection request specifically mentioning the podcast. Here's some real messages I've sent that have all been successful:

- "Hey Alice, I'd love to connect and see if it'd be a good fit to have you guest on my podcast to chat all things authority. Cheers, Alastair."

- "Hey Bob, great comment about authenticity! I'd love to have you come on my podcast to chat about this topic, would you be up for that? (No spammy messages to follow). Alastair."

- Hi Charlie, would you be interested in coming on my podcast The Recognized Authority to talk about thought leadership/ authority? I was just reading an article of yours about Zero Sigma, love to explore that & other ideas for my audience. (No spam to follow). — Alastair.

- Hey David. I'd love to invite you on my podcast to chat about mindset/attitude/stand up & consulting. Can we connect & see if it's a fit for you? No spammy crap to follow.

Many people comment that they appreciate the "No spammy messages" note, so I always include it — and never spam them afterwards!

The specific way I word this message may not be a good fit for you and that's fine. Make it your own. Reword it in your voice and allow your personality to show through.

21: Make a guest FAQ page

If you're bringing guests onto your podcast, then make their life easier by creating a "guest FAQ page" on your website to answer questions they might have about the podcast.

This will help them to figure out if your podcast is a good fit for them, and help them properly prepare for the interview.

Having the FAQ available can also save you a lot of time answering questions. I send the FAQ page link to potential guests early on in the conversation, after they agree in principle to the idea of coming on.

Who is the podcast aimed at?

Tell the guest who your ideal listener is, and who else might be listening. For example, my podcast *The Recognized Authority* is aimed at independent consultants, but I know that other professionals like accountants, business coaches, and even lawyers listen to it. I include this information on my guest

FAQ page as it will help the prospective guest figure out if they'd be a good fit for the podcast.

What questions will you ask during the podcast?

Most guests prefer to have some idea what they're going to be asked about, so give them some examples of the questions they might be asked on the show.

Who else has been a guest?

Listing other guests that they know reassures your guests that you and your show are legitimate.

How long will it take?

It's good for them to understand the time-commitment in advance so they can schedule it properly.

Will you record video or just audio?

It's good to let them know in advance if they're going to be on video, as people like to prepare for that. They might want to tidy their office, change their shirt, or put on make-up, and knowing about this in advance is less stressful than finding out just before recording.

Can they repurpose the podcast audio?

I like to explicitly mention that I encourage the guests to reuse the audio and video any way they like, because I want to get it in front of as wide an audience as possible.

How popular is the podcast/how much exposure will they get?

The "elephant in the room": how many listeners do you have? Higher profile guests want to know this to know if it's worthwhile coming on your podcast.

Aside: I think it's almost always worthwhile going on another podcast, even those with a tiny audience, because of the relationship you build with the host, and the experience you gain from talking about your topic to a different person.

Like everyone, when I started out I had a tiny audience, and so in my answer I addressed that directly, and then talked about the target audience and the promotion I was doing:

> This is not the podcast for you if you're looking for huge numbers. Look for

a consumer focused podcast if that's your thing. That said, we do have a very targeted audience of consultants and owners of small professional services firms. For promotion, we have a combined social media following of over 15,000 (multiple Twitter accounts, 5k+ on LinkedIn, Facebook etc). Every episode is promoted to these channels. We also invest in paid promotion.

Other questions you can answer

1. Do they need any special equipment or software?
2. Is explicit language acceptable on the show?
3. When will the episode be published?
4. How do they apply to be a guest?

Start off by answering the questions you think are important, and then add more questions into the FAQ as you are asked them by potential guests.

You can see an example podcast Guest FAQ page by visiting the online resources page here: **rec.nz/resources**

PART 5: Running Your Podcast

22: Document your workflow

Podcasts have a lot of moving parts, from show notes to cover-art, from scheduling interviews to editing, from transcripts to promotion.

You can release a handful of episodes without having a specific workflow, but if you're in this for the long haul then having a documented workflow will make your life easier, and the same for anyone that helps you with the podcast.

First, figure out what works for you

For your first few episodes, you'll be figuring things out. Experiment with different approaches and tweak your processes. Keep things as simple as you can at the start, and as you get more experienced you can add in more and more steps, but to start.

Make a checklist or SOP

Once your process is somewhat standardized, make

a checklist or SOP (Standard Operating Procedure) document. If you have external assistance with your podcast, you ask them to help document the procedure. This makes it easy for you to follow the steps yourself or delegate it to someone else if needed.

Example workflow

To give you an example of a more complex workflow for an established podcast, here's the workflow for *The Recognized Authority*, which is an interview format podcast with over a hundred episodes:

Pre-recording

- I invite the guest via *LinkedIn* messaging (I give them the Guest FAQ and Interview Scheduling links)
- The guest schedules onto calendar and is sent to intake form
- The guest completes the intake form

Editing

- We record the interview
- I message the editor to let him know a new interview is ready for edit
- The editor downloads the interview files from

recording service

- The editor selects 3-5 clips as options for the cold open and sends them to me
- I listen to these options and tell the editor which one I prefer
- The editor creates the full version of the episode audio which he calls *Guest Name v1.0* (if we make changes later we increment that number to *v1.1, v1.2* etc so we can track the latest version)
- For security, the editor creates a backup copy of all his work on the episode and uploads it to my *Google Drive*

The editor uploads the audio file to *Auphonic* for leveling, which makes sure all voices are at the same volume

Post-editing automation

- Automated: *Zapier* copies the audio file from *Auphonic* to *Google Drive* for later upload
- Automated: *Zapier* copies the audio file from *Auphonic* to *Otter* which creates an automated transcript
- Automated: *Zapier* copies the audio file from *Auphonic* to *Dropbox* - this is just another another backup

Optional: additional editing

- Optional: I sometimes do a “sanity check”

by listening to the completed episode — after 50 episodes I stopped doing this for the most part

- Optional: We make any necessary edits and rename the file to *v1.1* etc

Publishing

- My podcast producer copies the episode title that the guest suggested from the guest intake form and puts it into our show notes spreadsheet
- She also creates a draft episode description
- Optional: I rewrite the episode title if necessary
- I write or edit the episode description
- I choose 2-3 guest quotes from the transcription that we'll feature in promotion as quote images and in the episode description text
- My podcast producer creates the episode graphics, which consist of a square cover image for the podcast player, a rectangle cover image for social media, and two square quote images for social media
- She reviews and fixes any major errors in the automated transcription
- She also pull outs show notes mentions of books, websites and other references to link in the show notes
- She schedules the episode on our website
- She uploads the episode audio to the podcast host and schedules it for publishing

Promotion

- After it publishes, my producer emails the guest the episode link, promotional text, and graphics
- She posts the episode to *Twitter* and *LinkedIn*, and adds it into our social media rotation

That's the entire workflow for an episode of Season 1 of *The Recognized Authority.*

My first piece of advice: **don't panic**. *(Thanks, Douglas Adams!)*

If you're producing a solo podcast your episodes will be much simpler to produce.

The second thing I want you to notice is that, while there are a lot of steps in this workflow, look at how many pieces I'm personally involved in:

1. **inviting the guest**
2. **conducting the interview**
3. telling the editor there's a new interview (could be automated)
4. selecting a cold open clip (could be automated)
5. writing the description (could be delegated)
6. choosing the quotes (could be delegated)

You can see that I could reduce my workload to

just the first two steps, and even at a crunch I could delegate the invitations — but I don't want to do that because I like the networking benefit of those conversations.

I even know a podcaster who delegates the entire show, including hiring a professional podcast host.

This is your show. **You choose** how much you want to do, and automate or delegate the rest.

23: Don't burn out on editing

Podcast editing is time consuming and energy sapping.

It can be *particularly* draining when you're not used to listening to your own voice.

Recordings of your own voice always sound terrible to you because you normally hear it with the bone of your skull and jaw conducting the soundwaves to your ears. That's why you sound so different on tape.

The good news is that you can get used to hearing your own voice, but it does take quite some time. When you're editing yourself, listening to the sound of your voice, and often for the first time noticing just how many filler words you use, it can make for a tough experience.

If you add into the mix that you may be using an unfamiliar editing tool, trying to structure a podcast episode, and get things like levels right, it can be a lot to take on. And that's after all the effort and energy it took just to get the episode recorded in the first place!

I have two recommendations, depending on your situation.

Delegate editing to a professional

The first option is to delegate editing to someone else, ideally a professional podcast editor. You can find these online in podcast groups and on the usual freelancer websites.

They'll provide different levels of service from services that will provide turn-key production from the pre-planning stages, down to freelancers who will do basic editing only. You choose how much hand-holding you want on content planning and production.

Skip the editing step completely

The other option is to avoid editing altogether by recording "live to tape". The best way I know to do this is livestreaming. This is a more advanced option and it may not be for everyone, but if you go live when you record your podcast, when it's done, it's done!

If you make mistakes or stumble over words, all of it goes on the podcast. But that's okay! Set expectations by telling the listener that you're recording live, and they're getting everything raw and unedited.

If you do it live, there are other considerations. Live interviews means you probably need to have a regular time slot.

You need to decide whether to take questions from the audience and which platforms to stream on, like *Facebook*, *Instagram Live*, *LinkedIn*, *Twitch*, *YouTube*, and others.

You can also take advantage of technology to livestream to multiple channels — known as "multistreaming" — with a tool like *StreamYards* or *Restream*.

You can find an up-to-date list of livestreaming tools on the online resources page here: **rec.nz/resources**

24: Get ahead of your schedule

One of the most stressful aspects of publishing a regular podcast is when you realize you don't have the next episode ready and your publish date is looming!

When it comes to the production schedule, I like to get a few weeks ahead and stay ahead.

With the pre-produced show — as opposed to a livestream show — I typically have 5-8 weeks of episodes at various stages of production so that I can take some time off and not miss a week.

With livestreaming, the production workflow changes a little bit and typically the lead-time is shorter, with episodes released on the podcast feed just a week or two after being recorded on the live broadcast. It is easier though, because there is usually no editing step required when publishing a livestreamed episode to the podcast feed. I talk about livestreaming a bit more in the bonus chapter "Podcasting for authority" at the end of the book.

Stay organized

Podcasts have a lot of moving parts, so it's important to keep track of them all. You can use a project management tool like *Asana*, *ClickUp*, *Trello*, or even a shared spreadsheet. It doesn't matter how it's done so long as you have a system you and your team can use effectively.

We use a simple *Google* spreadsheet that's shared with both my audio editor and my assistant who takes care of show notes, graphics, and actually publishing the episode.

That spreadsheet helps my team and I stay on the same page, so we all know what guests are scheduled for recording, what's already recorded, and what's currently in the editing pipeline.

That means we try to have several weeks' worth of extra episodes already recorded and at various stages of the production process.

Save an evergreen episode

Sometimes life just happens, and you can't get your episode out this week. One thing that you can do to help in this scenario is to have an evergreen episode already recorded and ready to publish.

I have an evergreen solo episode of *The Recognized Authority* with audio file, episode art, and shownotes all ready to go if my regular episode can't go out for some reason.

Make guest outreach a regular habit

First, you should be reaching out to new potential guests on a regular basis.

The networking aspect is a huge benefit of podcasting so you should be doing this regardless of schedule — there is no better LinkedIn connection request than "I'd love to have you on my podcast".

If your podcast is weekly, record 2-3 interviews a week, every week for a month. That will get you around 6 weeks ahead of your publishing schedule.

At that point, you can choose to record one episode every week, or you can take a break for a month and then do another cluster of recordings. A hundred episodes in, I'm still finding my recording cadence, but I think I like batching them up a bit so I have busier months and quieter months.

25: Transcribe your episodes

A transcript is the audio of the podcast turned into text. Having the text of the episode helps in several ways:

- it can help you write your show notes
- it can help you repurpose your podcast into different content formats
- it's great for search engine optimization (SEO) which can put your content in front of new audiences
- and most importantly, it makes your audio accessible to people with hearing impairments

It also helps with creating the show notes and the links & resources section of the episode page, which can be a surprisingly difficult task!

There are two options for transcription.

Machine transcription

Machine transcription is where your audio is processed by a computer that outputs text usually at 90-95% accuracy.

Human transcription

Human transcription is where your audio is listened to by a real person who then transcribes it. The advantage of human transcription is the output text is at a higher accuracy, typically 98-99%.

Transcription tools & services

Otter.AI offers automated machine translation, and this is what I use for all my podcasts, as well as for transcribing our group calls. In fact, I have *Otter* connected directly to *Zoom* so it automatically transcribes all recordings.

REV.com offers incredibly fast human transcription which I've used and found to be of very high quality standards. They also offer automated machine translation — I haven't used this.

Descript is an all-in-one audio & video editor that also does machine transcription. I've found it tricky to use with interview episodes due to having more than one audio track, but it's absolutely fantastic for solo episodes.

There are a whole host of other tools and services including *GoTranscript*, *Scribie*, *Temi*, *TranscribeMe*, *Transcription Panda*. I haven't used these personally so I can't speak to them.

You can also find freelancers willing to do transcription and more on the usual freelancer & jobs marketplaces like *Upwork*, *Fiverr*, *Freelancer.com*, *OnlineJobs.PH*, and more.

26: Automate everything possible

You can classify work to be done into these three categories:

1. Work that must be done by YOU
2. Work that must be done by a human
3. Work that can be automated

You've got no choice about doing the category one work: it's on you. But that's okay, and even a good thing. In fact, I recommend spending as much time as possible in category one, as doing what *only you* can do is the most valuable thing you can do with your time.

The work in category two needs a human being's attention, and oftentimes that human will be you. Especially at the start. But the more you can offload this work, delegating and outsourcing it to others, the better. This is where you trade money for time, buying back your hours so that you can spend them on more valuable (category one!) tasks.

The good news is that there's a whole other category of tasks that are ideally suited for computers to take care of for us. Podcasting goes hand in hand with automation as producing a podcast includes many repetitive tasks for each new episode.

I know that these need a time investment to set up at the start, but once you've set up these automations they will work tirelessly for you, episode after episode.

What to automate

There are many podcast tasks you can automate, this is just a sample:

Audio Levelling. I use a tool called Auphonic to process my audio files. It evens out volume differences between speakers, raises the overall volume to the podcast standard (so every episode is the same), and makes a high quality but small MP3 file that is ready to publish.

Transcriptions. When Auphonic finishes processing the audio file, it saves it to a folder that kicks off an automatic transcription with a tool called Otter, which does a machine transcription resulting in text with ~ 95% accuracy. Another option is to have it automatically sent for human transcription on Rev.com, that will give you a ~ 99%

accuracy, but at a higher cost.

Guest Scheduling. When a guest agrees to come on my podcast, I don't want to have a nine-email back and forth discussion to find a time that suits us both. I give them a calendar link that shows them date & time options, and most guests can find a time that suits them there.

When they book a time there, it creates an appointment on their calendar including a link to the recording studio, and more information about what to expect.

With higher profile guests you may need to work around their calendar availability a bit more, so it can be a more manual process.

Guest Intake Form. When a guest books onto the show, afterwards they are redirected to the guest intake form. This form asks for all the details needed from them to publish the podcast, including their name, bio, headshot, website & social links, etc.

Project Management. When a guest books, you can have that kick off an automation to create a task in Asana, ClickUp or some other project management tool. You can use task templates to automatically set up a checklist for everything that needs to be done for your episode.

Sharing Published Episodes. You can automatically share your podcast episodes when they're published by connecting up your social media accounts with your website or podcast host. I recommend being cautious about how you do this kind of automated sharing, as sometimes the output looks clearly automated. Test and see what works best for you.

Email or Slack Message. You can send an email or a Slack message to a guest, co-host or assistant when an episode goes live. This is great for kicking off promotional efforts or just keeping everyone in the loop.

Update a spreadsheet. An automatically populated spreadsheet is a great way to keep track of lists of data, from your episode URLs to make later sharing easier, to a list of every account username that mentions your podcast on Twitter, or every mention of a unique hashtag that you monitor for listener feedback.

Automation tools & resources

Automation tools are the "glue" between different components of your workflow. Here's some tools and resources to help you get started.

- *Zapier* is probably the most popular automation tool, and connects over 5,000 apps & services.

- *IFTTT* (*If This Then That*) is another tool that connects over 700 apps & services.

- *Automators* is a podcast that helps listeners to implement automation, they have a fantastic discussion forum where the community share tips and advice at talk.automators.fm

Start simple and build on it

I suggest you keep automation to a minimum when you're starting out so that you get used to your workflow, and build it over time.

Once you have a few episodes under your belt, start adding in automation and extra workflow steps to replace manual tasks.

Automation isn't perfect

Automation doesn't always give you a perfect result. Humans know how to tweak and adapt things to fit, computers will do exactly what you tell them and nothing more. This is a trade-off that we have to make, and often it's a 50-50 call.

I ask myself "what's best for the long term?" and sometimes that's automating a task even though I *know* the output will be imperfect, because that's better than doing the task some of the time perfectly, but forgetting to do it other times.

Run a backup recording during important interviews

If you're recording podcast interviews, you may only get one shot with a high-profile podcast guest, so you want to make sure you get it recorded first time.

If you use a good podcast recording service, it will have a built-in backup. But even if you use a service, it's nice to have your own backup recording running at the same time.

This was important for me when I interviewed one of the world's leading marketing consultants. We recorded on my favorite podcast recording service as usual, but I also turned on my backup recording, as I always do when I'm interviewing high-profile guests.

After we were done with the interview there was a glitch with the recording on the online service. It doesn't happen often, but it can happen.

But my backup recording was fine, and we used that for production, rather than being forced into an awkward conversation and asking the guest to do a second take.

Just to note, a couple of weeks later, the recording service found the bug in their system and were able to give me the original recordings.

I use a very simple solution for my backup

recording — I use the recording feature in Camtasia Studio, which is screen recording & editing software. When I'm recording a backup of an interview, I have it record my microphone, the "system audio" — which is my guest's audio — and the screen where the recording studio video is showing.

Have a backup connection

Again, if you have a high-profile guest you may only get one shot at the interview. In that case, it's good to have a backup solution in case your computer or internet connection goes down.

It doesn't need to be complicated, but it's good to have at least thought it through beforehand. For me, my backup connection is simply *Zoom* on my phone.

Document your automations

Automations are fantastic. When you've built enough automations and have them running for months they become something that *just happens*.

It's easy to forget where they are set up, what account is connected to what.

I suggest that you keep a list of them somewhere — for me that's in my primary "podcast workflow" spreadsheet.

PART 6: Growing Your Podcast

27: Make a podcast section on your website

When you publish your podcast, it will appear in podcast directories like Apple Podcasts, Spotify, Stitcher, and anywhere else you — or your podcast host — have submitted it.

It doesn't automatically get added to your business website unless you've taken some action to ensure it is published there.

This section has a lot of technical details but I'll address a couple of high-level questions you might have first.

Why put the podcast on the main business website instead of having a standalone website for the podcast?

This is debatable and from a technical viewpoint, it may be easier to set up a separate website for the podcast.

My take on it goes back to your goals for the podcast — if your goals include helping to market your business, create brand awareness and even generate leads, then I think it makes sense to put it on your primary business website. If you have different goals, you may have another take on this.

Many podcast hosts can provide a simple standalone website, why not use that?

Again, this is context-dependent, and I've even used one of those generated websites in the past because it allowed me to get a website spun up very quickly for the podcast.

But having the website on your own business site means:

- You can build your email list
- You have more control over the podcast's appearance
- You can include extra content like show notes, transcripts, videos images, and quotes
- You are getting the search engine optimization (SEO) benefits of having a podcast
- You are promoting your own brand instead of a podcast directory
- You can include comments, FAQs, bios, news or anything else you'd like to add to the website
- You can include sponsors and other monetization options like Patreon or

premium episodes

For me, these benefits outweigh the time and investment required to set up the podcast on your website.

That's WHY you should have a podcast section, here's WHAT you actually need. The two basic elements for a podcast website:

1. Podcast Episode Listing page

2. Podcast Individual Episode pages

Podcast Episode Listing Page

The Podcast Episode Listing Page is the centerpiece, it's the control center for your podcast on your website, the link you send out to people and that you put in your social media profiles. Quite often it's at example.com/podcast

As the main hub for the podcast, the Podcast Episode Listing Page has a number of elements that you can include:

The title of the podcast.

The podcast's main cover art.

A description of the podcast: a few paragraphs describing what the podcast is about, who it's for, and the benefits they will get from listening.

Links to the podcast on all of the major podcast platforms: there are a lot of different podcast platforms, so make it easy for your listeners to find your podcast by linking to it on the popular platforms. On my site, I link to Apple Podcasts, Spotify, Google Podcasts, Amazon, Stitcher, ACast, TuneIn, Pocket Casts, Deezer, Breaker, and the RSS feed. This isn't essential, but I'm a fan of anything that makes it easier for people to listen to my podcast.

A listing of all the episodes: I recommend listing the most recent episodes at the top. I like to include the episode number, episode title, a short teaser — I use the first 45 words from the episode description. Both the episode title and the "View Episode" button link to the individual episode page.

Here's what an episode listing looks like on my podcast listing page:

> EPISODE 50
> **How Content Can Save Your Business with Marcus Sheridan**
> Writing articles for your website or social media is hugely time-consuming, and it's so difficult to find the time when you're already working long hours on client projects. But you need to make the time. Here's why. In this episode, bestselling author & renowned speaker
> VIEW EPISODE →

If you have a lot of episodes and it becomes too hard to navigate, you may want to paginate — splitting the listing page up so that it lists only 25-50 episodes per page. This depends on page layout and also your website and hosting configuration. I have over 100 episodes on my episode listing page and it loads in around 1.2 seconds.

Optional sections for the podcast listing page

The podcast publishing schedule: it's nice to let your audience know when they can expect new episodes. I have "Publishes Weekly on Monday Mornings" under the cover art at the top of my podcast listing page.

Podcast host biography: create a human connection with your audience by including some information about the podcast host. I have a photo and a few short paragraphs of text describing who I am and why I created the podcast.

Podcast testimonials or reviews: if you get some positive reviews or testimonials for the podcast, you can put some of them on your podcast listing page. Remember, this is the page that helps newcomers decide if the podcast is worth listening to, and reading a testimonial or positive can help with that. I have only one testimonial listed on my podcast listing, but it's right at the top in large type so it's impossible to miss.

Podcast trailer video: if you've created a podcast

trailer, the episode listing page is a great place to showcase it! It will serve to introduce the podcast to the audience and give a

Podcast Individual Episode Pages

The Podcast Listing page showcases the whole podcast. The job of an Individual Episode page is to showcase a single episode.

Every episode you publish should get its own page.

A note on terminology: because podcast episodes are conceptually similar to blog posts, many people refer to individual episode pages as "posts". I tend to use the terms interchangeably, but for the sake of clarity here I'll refer to them as "individual episode pages".

The individual episode page is the online hub for that one episode, so it should have all the information a listener might want, links to any websites mentioned during the episode, links to books or other resources. Here's a full breakdown of what I like to include on a podcast individual episode page.

The title of the episode. I already addressed the issue of writing episode titles, check that out in Chapter 16 "Write great episode titles".

An embedded podcast player with the episode. This is something that all good podcast hosts will provide. They'll have some code that you can copy and paste into your website to embed the episode.

The show notes for the episode. This is a few paragraphs describing what this episode is about. Say who the guest is if it's an interview, and mention the topics you covered. The goal of the show notes is to entice people into listening to the episode.

A transcript of the episode. A transcript is your podcast episode in text format. Transcripts have many benefits so I've written in detail about them in Chapter 24.

Guest biography. A biography, typically called a "bio" is a concise paragraph of information that professionals use to introduce themselves. You can find short bios on social media and particularly on the About Page of the guest's website. I ask the guest for their bio in my intake form, so I copy and paste it from there into the episode page.

Links & resources. During a podcast episode, you or your guest might mention people, companies, books, websites or even other podcasts. Including links to all of the resources mentioned in the podcast gives your listeners a reason to visit the show notes page on your website, and is yet another reason for your guest to promote the podcast episode page.

Call to Action. No matter what your content is or where your audience is interacting with you, it's always a good idea to have a call to action ("CTA").

You are giving them a clear **next step** for them to take to embed further into your world. The call to action could be asking them to subscribe to your email list, listen to another podcast episode, or even read a related blog post.

Okay, so far in this section I covered WHY you should have a podcast section, and WHAT you actually need. Now let's talk about HOW to do it.

How to create the podcast section on your website

This will depend on the technology that you're using for your website. If your business is like many others, you use WordPress. If that's the case you have access to numerous options to add the podcast features you'll need.

The most common is to use a third-party plugin like PowerPress Podcasting, Seriously Simple Podcasting, or Fusebox — all of these have free options available at the time of writing.

What do I use? I've been developing websites in WordPress for nearly 20 years, and have a developer in-house, so we built our own — very simple — solution using Advanced Custom Fields.

A podcast trailer is great for testing

One other thing to note about building a podcast website is that it's much easier to do it if there's an actual episode already published to the feed, it lets you set up and test everything.

That's one major reason I like to publish a podcast trailer in advance. But don't worry if you've already launched the podcast, you can still create these pages after the fact!

28: Make it easy for guests to share

Ask any podcaster what their number one challenge is, and they'll tell you that it's growing the listenership.

If you have an interview podcast, you are lucky enough to have a natural "network effect" built-in, where you can ask your guests to share the podcast with their audience.

Go a step further than just asking your guests to share it — make it easy for them by providing text, images and even video for them to copy & paste into their social networks. Think of it as removing friction.

Write promotional text for them

Write some short text describing the episode and include hashtags, so that they can just copy & paste the whole thing into their social networks without having to think about it.

Individual episode artwork with their name & photo

Create a cover image for each episode with the guest name and episode title. You can even include a headshot photo of the guest if you ask them for that during intake.

Create quote images

Choose several interesting quotes from your guest's appearance on the podcast. As I mentioned in the *opening hook* section, a way to find these quotes more easily is to look for the guest's 3rd, 4th, or 5th answer in the interview.

Make images with the text of these quotes, including your guest's name and even their headshot. The image should be branded with your podcast, and you could even include a short URL directly to the episode. I use a template in Canva to make creating these quotes quick & easy.

Create video clips

The next level up from images is to create short video clips from the conversation. For guest promo clips I recommend the following format & content.

- Think about the content of the clip

  - Your guest sharing an important point will optimize for sharing
  - A back-and-forth conversation with you & your guest both making good points will optimize for authority building
- Make the clip around 30-90 seconds
- Square video for social shareability (1,080 pixels wide)
- Use the top 20% for a headline
- Use the bottom 20% for captions
- Use the middle 60% for your video

Delegate & outsource

It's vital to note that you don't have to do all of this work yourself, personally!

In fact it's better if you don't do this post-production work as it will tire you out and make "podfading" more likely. You can find podcast production services and individual freelancers who can take on these tasks at a range of different price points.

You can make the video file available somewhere like Google Drive so your guest can upload it directly to their social networks. Make sure the video includes your branding and information on where to find the full episode.

29: Build an email list

One of the downsides of podcasting is that you don't know who is listening to your show. It's a one-way relationship, and when someone listens to an episode you rarely get information more granular than just another download number showing up in your monthly analytics.

You own the relationship

An email list helps you change that by inviting your listeners onto a platform that you own completely. If your listeners opt-in to your list they are putting their hand up and asking you to contact them.

The benefit of getting them onto your email list is you're not "building on rented ground" by growing a following on a social media platform that can — and have — changed their rules or pulled the plug.

Email service providers

To build an email list, you'll need an email

service provider like *ActiveCampaign*, *ConvertKit*, or *Mailchimp*. I've used all three of these at various times. *ConvertKit* is my favorite and what I use now due to its combination of powerful features and simple user interface at its core.

There are plenty of other options, most of them with similar functionality, but if you're just getting started then I'd recommend going with *ConvertKit* or *ActiveCampaign*.

Gaining subscribers

Once you've committed to building an email list, you'll want to actually attract people to sign up or "subscribe". To achieve that, you need to put an incentive in front of them, ideally something that is useful and compelling.

"Sign up for our free email newsletter" just won't cut it as it sounds like you're going to send them boring company news once a quarter.

Offer them a free resource that helps them solve their problem. It doesn't have to solve their problem completely, just move them towards the solution. This opt-in incentive is often referred to as a "lead magnet" in the marketing world.

I really like checklists and cheatsheets as they are quick to consume and quick to create. Email courses are great — I use this on *The Recognized*

Authority where I offer a free 7-day email course to help experts build their authority. You could also offer access to an exclusive video, webinar replay, interview or ebook.

Just be careful you don't try to pack too much value into your lead magnet. If it's too large it may be overwhelming to consume and may trigger "I'll save this for later", where later never arrives!

Tell them about it

Once you have your email list and opt-in incentive set up then it's time to start telling your audience about it. Put it on regular rotation in your social media posts, and mention it on every podcast episode.

30: Experiment with paid ads when you start

Ask any podcaster what their number one difficulty is and they'll all answer the same: "growing our audience".

In fact, much of the advice in this book is aimed at helping you grow your audience, making it easier for you, your guests, and your listeners to promote the podcast.

It's hardest to grow at the start

For folks without a huge audience already, the hardest time to grow the podcast is right at the beginning.

That's when you don't have a lot of episodes. It means you don't have a body of work to demonstrate consistency. It means you don't have a large number of past guests sharing their own episodes and others from your podcast. It means you don't have Google and SEO working for you. It means you don't have a lot of current listeners sharing your episodes with others.

If you have the budget for it, now is a good time to experiment with paid advertising to jump-start your audience growth. Audience growth compounds over time, so giving yourself a boost at the beginning can pay dividends further down the road.

Generic paid traffic

There are plenty of generic paid traffic options from social media platforms like LinkedIn, Facebook, Twitter, and Instagram to search engines like Google and Bing.

These are very popular systems and you'll find a lot of books and guides available to help you figure those out. My only advice about the bigger paid networks is to think very carefully about how to prevent your ads from appearing in front of people who probably won't be interested in your podcast, so you don't waste your ad spend.

Paid advertising in podcast apps

Another option that I've used is to advertise to podcast listeners directly in podcast apps. There are several options including *Spotify*, *Overcast*, *Podcast Addict*, *Pocket Casts*, and *PlayerFM*.

You'll typically have fewer targeting options in

these apps than you'd have in the larger platforms, but the advantage is you know you're advertising directly to people who already listen to podcasts, and they can easily subscribe with one click.

Real-life costs

To give you some real numbers, I advertised *The Recognized Authority* in *Overcast* and *Podcast Addict* in several different categories from Business to Education to History. A spend of $2,000 USD resulted in over 1 million ad views, 5,700 ad clicks, and 174 subscribers — that's a cost-per-subscriber of around $11.50 USD.

The most expensive category was *Podcast Addict's* Business category, which was $36 per subscriber, and the least expensive was *Overcast's* Education category at $6.50 per subscriber.

If you have a budget, I'd recommend experimenting with these ads until you find something that works for you. Watch the price per category: most podcast apps with ads have the pricing on their website, it varies depending on category and demand.

31: Promote by guesting elsewhere

One of the best ways to expand your audience and attract listeners to your podcast is to guest on other people's podcasts.

Why you should guest on podcasts

When you are invited onto another podcast, it's a vote of confidence. The host is indicating to their loyal group of followers that they trust you enough to bring you onto their platform and spend time speaking with you.

It's easy for listeners to subscribe to your podcast as they are already in their podcasting app. When you mention your podcast name, it's easy for them to search for it and try an episode.

Guesting on podcasts gives you a lot of social media content to share. Once the episode airs, the host will almost always promote it on their social media channels, giving you content to reshare. They'll often create specific episode assets like quote images, cover images and even videos that you can share.

Most podcasts you guest on will also link to your social media profiles and your website. These “backlinks” are valuable and will help boost your website ranking in the search engines.

How to guest on podcasts

Unfortunately the cat is out of the bag — everyone and their mother knows that podcast guesting is one of the fastest, most effective ways to build authority and grow your audience. You’ll see this advice everywhere. It’s still good advice, it’s just that it’s far more competitive than it used to be.

There is good news. If you’re reading this book, you’re probably intending to launch a podcast and there is no single better way to get invited on podcasts than to have your own podcast!

Start your podcast, and invite other podcasters on as guests. Many of these will reciprocate and have you appear on their show.

There are also outreach services that help to place guests on podcasts. I’m wary of these as many of them seem to be playing a numbers game.

How to pitch yourself as guest

When you launch your podcast you'll start to receive a lot of unsolicited emails suggesting guests for your show. These emails tend to be a fantastic guide in how you should not pitch yourself to other podcasts.

If you are pitching to appear as a guest, I recommend inviting the host onto your podcast first and asking them if they think you might be a good fit for their show in your post-interview chat.

If you're pitching a podcast without having the host on your show, then I recommend that you establish some kind of relationship with them first, following them on social media, engaging with their posts and connecting with them.

Only after you've created some rapport, then contact them. With your contact message demonstrate that you know their podcast topic, format and audience.

If you can show that you know what the podcast is about, and what their listeners care about, you're already ahead of 90% of guest pitches.

If you can also reference an in-joke or something mentioned in a recent episode so they know you've actually listened to an episode, you're ahead of 99% of your competition.

Suggested episode topics or even suggestions for the episode title are useful for podcast hosts to get a flavour of what you talk about and whether it would be useful for their listeners.

Show up ready

When you are invited on, show up prepared, and on time. Do the preparatory work like listening to an episode or two, checking out the podcast website and the hosts' social media channels. Think about what topics might be useful for the podcast audience, and how you can deliver as much value as possible. If you focus on helping the podcast audience, that will build a lot of credibility with the host too.

Call to action

When you guest on another podcast, I recommend one of two options for the call to action:

1. Ask the listener to check out your podcast.
2. Offer the listener a free gift of some kind.

Telling them about your podcast is a great option for several reasons. Firstly, they're already in a podcast app so it's a smaller effort to find your podcast than to do something else like check out your website. Secondly, since they're already a podcast listener there's a good chance that they might become a regular listener to your podcast.

The other option is a free gift and the goal here

is to have them sign up to your email list. This is often referred to as a lead magnet. The advantage of this option is that you get their direct contact information and you can learn who they are, rather than just another number in your podcast analytics.

Read more about calls to action in chapter 19.

32: Create a media one-sheet

The humble one-sheet goes by many names: one-sheet, one-pager, media kit or press kit, but its purpose is simple. It's usually a one- or two-page overview & representation of an individual or organisation.

Your one-sheet gives a clear snapshot of you and your business, allowing you to quickly communicate the most important elements of your message. It should pique the interest of media, podcast hosts, event organizers, agents, and anyone else who might be able to give you publicity or a platform.

Even the process of creating a one-sheet will help you clarify your positioning and messaging.

Once it's created it will help you save time by having all your most important information all in one place to send to interested parties like podcast hosts and event organizers.

Elements to include

Put everything that might be relevant to an interviewer or event organizer in your one-sheet, including:

Your Name

Include your name as you would like it to appear in promotional materials.

Contact Information

Your contact information should be front and center, make it easy for people to get in touch with you to invite you to speak, guest, or even to work with you.

Positioning Statement

A positioning statement is a simple statement defines your brand position, identifies your ideal customer and the problem you solve for them. I like to keep things simple with a template like "I help these people solve this problem (or get this result)." Your positioning statement will evolve over time, so make a note to update your one-sheet on a regular basis.

Short & Long Biography

Your "bio" is a quick summary used to introduce you, and is often read out verbatim by podcast hosts and event MCs. It can be useful to have a short version that is a couple of sentences in length, and a longer one that has more detail.

Professional Headshot & Publicity Photos

Whether you're speaking at an event, guesting on

a podcast, or even simply writing a guest article, you will almost always need to provide a headshot for the organizers to use in promotional materials. Make it easy by including a square, high quality headshot photograph. As a rule-of-thumb, I go with 1000x1000 pixels as the minimum size to provide if it's being used online. If you're being featured in print then they may need larger sizes.

Social Profiles

Don't forget to link to all of your active social media accounts on your one-sheet.

Publications — Books, Podcast, Videos, etc

If you have written books, host a podcast, or made videos, list them here. Include titles, ISBN and cover images if you can, as well as links to where they can be found.

Speaking Topics, Talking Points & Sample Interview Questions

Your one-sheet is all about making it easy for media, podcasters, and event bookers to put you on their platform. Including information like talking points and sample questions helps them to get a feel for what you talk about, and some will even use the questions verbatim — so make sure you're prepared for them!

Speaking & Guest Appearances

Including a list of events you've spoken at, your podcast guest appearances, and other media appearances brings huge social proof & credibility.

Endorsements, Testimonials & Accolades

Add high-lights from endorsements & client testimonials that you have received, this is more social proof and helps to build credibility & trust.

Media Logos

Recognizable "as seen in" logos create trust. Include logos from any media you have appeared or been referenced in. This can include TV, radio, print, blogs, podcasts, and events where you've been highlighted.

Client Logos

When you include client logos you're showing the viewer that you are trusted by these organizations.

Industry Association Logos

By including logos from industry associations that you are part of, this shows that you are an active member of your industry.

Quotes

Writers and publishers are often under time pressure to meet a deadline. One way to help those who don't have time to interview you is to include some quotes — from yourself — in your one-sheet for them to use verbatim.

Additional Resources

Include links to anything that isn't covered by any of the sections above, but might still be useful to the reader.

Call to Action

End your one-sheet by giving the reader a clear next step to follow. That's usually to contact you, your assistant or booking agent, but you can make it whatever feels most appropriate for your situation. The key is that your call to action is clear, concise, and easy for them to follow.

Make it visually appealing

A good one-sheet is concise, visually appealing, and easy to scan read. Use your brand colors & fonts to keep it congruent with the rest of your brand & visual identity.

It's good to have it available as a web page so you can email a link, as a PDF that you can attach, or both. Remember that someone may be looking at a printout rather than an online version, so it's a good idea to spell out contact information as well as including a link.

Tools to create your one-sheet

You can create your one-sheet in many different ways including word processors like Word or Google Docs, a graphics tool like Canva, or a web page builder like Elementor.

I built my one-sheet directly as a web page,

you can see it by visiting the resources page at **rec.nz/resources**

Make it easy to find

However you create your one-sheet, make sure it's easily found on your website.

It doesn't need to be in your primary navigation menu at the top of the website; I think a good place to put it is the website footer menu at the bottom of every page.

PART 7: The Number One Mistake

33: Don't screw up by not starting

There's a lot of podcast strategy & technical advice in this book and elsewhere. But the most important thing I can tell you is this: don't let the details get in your way.

It's very easy to get stuck in the weeds, obsessing over equipment or strategy. Don't let perfect be the enemy of the good. Just. Start.

If you take nothing else from this book, remember this: if you want to start a podcast, at some point you will need to hit the record button and start talking!

Guinness World Record?

I may be the unwitting owner of a Guinness World Record for the "Longest Time to Start a Podcast".

I first started planning a podcast in July 2014, and it pains me to say that it took nearly 7 years before I actually launched *The Recognized Authority* in April of 2021. There were good reasons for delay, but when I think how much further I'd be now if I had started

3 or 4 years earlier, I regret it.

Why do we delay putting ourselves out there?

I interviewed acclaimed keynote speaker & best-selling author Marcus Sheridan. Marcus is an expert in growing businesses through publishing and content-creation.

I asked him why he thinks so few people create content and publish their thinking, given how hugely effective it is in building authority and creating new business.

> "The fact of the matter is many people will not do what it takes to be successful in becoming the thought leader in their space.
> Too many are playing the victim card, but are — if we're being very honest — just being lazy. Sometimes they create a bunch of red tape that shouldn't be there. There's a lot of excuses that we make, I've seen them all.
> You say things like I'm a one man army. But as a one person army you can do more, because you have no board of supervisors, you have no attorneys to go

> through. You can just create, you can be a digital David in a land of Goliaths."
> **— Marcus Sheridan, on *The Recognized Authority*, Episode 50** rec.nz/50

Given the fact that you're reading a book, I suspect you may not be one of the lazy ones — but instead you may need to beware perfectionism & self-made constraints, like overplanning.

Your first episode may not be a sublime, award-winning podcast episode. Nor the second, nor the third. But every time you record, edit, and publish it will improve, and in a relatively short period of time you'll realize that you've got something you're proud of creating.

The only way you can really screw up your podcast is by not starting. Everything else can be fixed as you go.

BONUS CHAPTER: Podcasting for authority

This bonus chapter outlines a specific plan to help you create a podcast that builds your authority in the most optimal, accelerated way possible.

Building authority is slow, podcasting accelerates the process

Two of my three podcasts have the word "authority" in the title, because for several years, I've been going deeper and deeper down the rabbit hole on how building authority works. I've been picking apart the building blocks that make up authority, and learning how an expert can become recognized in their field.

One of the biggest takeaways from my research and client work is just how effective podcasting can be a means to build authority, even without trying to optimize for it.

If you do optimize your approach to your podcast, you can accelerate the authority building process significantly.

This is crucial because building authority is slow, measured in years, not months.

Building authority and exercising have a lot in common

- If you go to the gym a couple of times for one week, that won't have any impact.
- Do it for a quarter and you'll start to feel different.
- Do it for a 12 months and it will have a dramatic, positive impact.
- Make it a regular life-long habit, and it will change your life.

The building-blocks of authority

Experts build authority by creating a "body of work" in a specific field.

Consistently creating and publishing helpful content over a period of time helps you develop your point of view, grow your audience, and build your credibility & trust with them.

1. **Consistency** builds trustworthiness and allows your audience to make your content part of their routine.

2. **Publishing** means you take the risk of putting your work out into the world, instead of keeping it to yourself, and this builds respect and trust.

3. **Helpful content** actually helps your audience with the problem that they're facing.

4. **Significant period of time** is required to build a wide audience, build relationships, and create a body of work of sufficient size.

Podcasting is tailor-made for building authority

When I asked my *Authority Labs* mastermind group what they found most difficult about building authority, the answer was unanimously "finding the time to write & publish".

But as we've already seen in quotes from Chris Do and Marcus Sheridan, you simply must find the time — or make the time — to publish content. Otherwise you will remain unknown.

If we take the four building blocks of "consistency", "publishing", "helpful content", and "over time", podcasting actually helps achieve all of these in one go.

1. **Consistency.** Podcasts have a regular

publishing schedule built-in from the start.

2. **Publishing.** Also built-in from the start, podcasts are designed to publish your content and distribute it directly to the ears of your audience.

3. **Helpful content.** A podcast that isn't helpful to its target audience won't succeed, so you have to figure this part out. You're on the right track if you're reading this!

4. **Significant period of time.** A successful podcast can run for years, and the good news is that you can minimize how much time you need to spend on it personally down to just a couple of hours a month.

Optimizing your podcast for authority

What I've said so far is applicable to *every* business podcast, and even if you have a different goal for your podcast, e.g. business development or audience growth, you'll almost certainly still end up building authority as a side-effect.

However, if your primary goal for the podcast is to build your authority, there are a number of strategic decisions you can make to accelerate that process.

Hybrid format

If you use a hybrid podcast format with ~50% interviews, ~50% solo episodes, you gain the distribution & credibility-by-association benefits of doing guest interviews, along with the personal authority benefit of a having a solo show.

Release weekly

A weekly release schedule optimizes both for creating significant amounts of content, and for audience adoption of your podcast into their weekly routine.

The future is video

My advice: record video as well as audio.

Audio doesn't share well on social media, and in fact most social platforms won't allow you to upload audio files directly. With no visual component combined with most social users browsing with sound off, audio-only content simply doesn't "stop the scroll".

Video is a whole different story. Social media user behavior is driving demand for video and the social platforms making big changes in order to better support short-form video in particular. *TikTok* and *Instagram* are getting all the press, but *YouTube* is still quietly dominating the video space [*Pew Research*].

Video is hard, and recording solo episodes to camera is even harder. It will take you some time to figure out lighting and improve your delivery, but this knowledge and experience will prove invaluable for you as you build your authority and are invited to events and other shows.

Don't bother with audiograms

Audiograms are videos that have been generated from audio files. They don't include footage of the speakers, instead showing a moving soundwave, and usually the captions for the video.

The problem with audiograms is that in my experience — and that of other podcasters I've spoken to about this — they tend to get significantly less engagement and reach than videos featuring camera footage of actual people speaking.

If you have an unlimited budget, they might be worth doing, but for most smaller business podcasts I simply wouldn't bother with audiograms.

Publish full episode videos to YouTube

As podcasters who want to build authority, we should be publishing full episodes to *YouTube*.

Now, I realise that the very next thing an

experienced podcaster will say is "hang on, that means we need to completely change our editing process".

Yes. If you're publishing video to YouTube, that does have significant implications for editing. Effectively, we're editing in a video editing tool, rather than in an audio editor.

That brings in extra cost, equipment and time requirements. Is it worthwhile? I spoke to Megan Dougherty from the podcast production agency *One Stone Creative* about this.

> "A shocking number of people listen to podcasts on YouTube. They just play the videos in the background, listening to it while they're going about their day. I thought there's no way that it makes sense for YouTube to be used in this way as a podcast delivery format, but then we did the math, and the math said I was wrong. Yes, you should absolutely be putting your episodes on YouTube, according to data"
> **— Megan Dougherty, on *The Recognized Authority*, Episode 73 rec.nz/73**

One Stone Creative releases a report based on their research on business podcasts every year —

it's linked from the online resources page here: **rec.nz/resources**

Livestreaming

Rather than editing video, there is another option, but it's even more daunting than video for many, and that is livestreaming.

If you livestream your episodes you can record them "live to tape", negating the need for editing. You can tell the audience at the start of the show that it's being recorded live, and ask for their tolerance for any glitches and missteps.

There are two schools of thought on where you should publish your full episodes on *YouTube*. One option is to create a podcast playlist on your main *YouTube* channel. The other option is to create a separate podcast channel dedicated to the podcast. Both have pros and cons, I prefer the dedicated channel but it's not a showstopper if you go with a playlist on your main channel.

Create short-form video clips

You can take the full-size episode video and edit it down into a number of 30-90 second short clips. This allows you to take advantage of the distribution boost video is getting right now. Having these short-form clips available to release on a daily basis will have a huge acceleration effect on your audience growth.

I wrote more about the specific format of these that I'd recommend you use earlier in the book in the section on video.

Repurpose video clips as text, images & carousels

Short video clips are ideal for repurposing into other formats like quote images, text posts, and carousels. For these fragmented pieces of content, make the call to action for the consumer to go check out the full episode.

Publish this content daily on social media. This is a critical part of the process — you've done all the hard work of creating content, now it's time to put it out into the world.

Batching and delegation

Use batching to optimize your workflow when it comes to planning and recording solo episodes. Don't forget to use scheduling tools, whether third-party social content management tools or the built-in content schedulers in your social media platforms.

Delegate as much of this as possible: in-house, to third-party services, or to a virtual assistant.

In an ideal world, you will turn up for the recording, and someone else takes care of the rest of the details. For most of us, that's not realistic, especially in the early days, but it does help.

Leverage your podcast to guest on others

The word has been out for quite some time now: podcast guesting is hugely effective in growing an audience and building authority. It seems like everyone is recommending that you get on podcasts as a guest.

I wholeheartedly agree with them. But it's not easy, because everyone else is trying to get on podcasts as a guest too! That means that experienced podcasters have their defenses on high alert, and are simply rejecting the vast majority of guest pitches.

But there's a very simple way to build a great relationship with a podcast host — invite them to be a guest on your podcast!

That allows you to build rapport and trust with them. Once you've gotten to know them, ask if they think you'd be a good fit to come on their show. In fact, if you do a good job, they may even ask you that before you even broach the subject.

Summary

Having your own podcast solves multiple problems that experts encounter on the road to building authority. It can massively accelerate your progress on that journey if you make the right choices in your setup.

You will still need to put in the effort, particularly in setting up and learning how to do video. But once you have things set up, you can delegate most of the work and reduce your personal time commitment down to a minimum, while still achieving your goals.

Appendix 1: Glossary of podcasting terms

Audacity. A popular free audio editing software used by many podcasters.

Audio interface. A device that connects your microphone to your computer. It allows you to adjust gain, and often boosts the signal, reducing noise and helping to capture high-quality audio. You need an audio interface if you use a microphone that does not have a USB connector.

Audiogram. A video that showcases a snippet of your episode; it displays a soundwave for the visual element of the video.

Clipping. Clipping occurs when the volume of an audio signal is too high and exceeds the maximum capacity of the recording equipment, causing a distorted or crunchy sound. The name comes from the audio waveform looking"clipped" off at the top and bottom. You can avoid it by turning down the gain on your microphone. See gain.

Co-host. A buddy who joins the host and helps guide the conversation.

Compression. A technique used to make audio files smaller, without sacrificing quality.

EQ (Equalization). Balancing the different frequencies in an audio file, to make sure everything sounds just right.

Editing. Cleaning up the audio, stitching in any required pieces like an intro or outro, and making sure everything sounds polished and professional.

Episode. Each podcast is broken down into individual episodes, like chapters in a book. Each episode has its own topic and theme, so you can pick and choose which ones you want to listen to.

Episode description. A written summary of what was talked about in an episode that is included alongside the audio in podcast apps. See "show notes".

Feed. A way to subscribe to a podcast and automatically get new episodes as they come out. No more manually checking for updates!

Gain. The gain control increases or decreases the sensitivity of the microphone, which in turn affects the volume of the recorded audio. If the gain is set too low, the audio may sound too quiet. If the gain is set too high, the audio may sound distorted or clipping.

Host. The person who leads the conversation and keeps the show going. "Host" can also refer to the podcast hosting company (see below).

ID3 tags. Tiny bits of information that are added to an MP3 file, like the title, artist, year, and genre.

Intro and Outro. The opening and closing music and announcements for each episode.

MP3. The most common audio file format used for podcast episodes.

Microphone. The device that turns your voice into an audio file. Without it, you wouldn't be able to make a podcast.

Mixer. A device that blends multiple audio sources together, like your voice and background music. Mixers typically have inputs for microphones, musical instruments, and other audio sources, as well as controls for adjusting volume, tone, and other aspects of the audio. Mixers can be used in podcasting to ensure that audio sources are balanced and that the final audio output sounds clear and professional. These are particularly useful when recording conversations with multiple people in the same room.

Normalization. Making sure all the audio in an episode is at the same volume level. This is very helpful when you have more than one person speaking on a podcast.

Podcast. An audio show that you can download and listen to on the go. Typically a series of episodes.

Podcast app. An app on your phone or computer that lets you play and organize your podcast episodes.

Podcast hosting. A service that stores your podcast audio files, so you don't have to worry about technical stuff.

Podfade. A term used in the podcasting world to describe when a podcast loses its momentum and stops being regularly produced and published. "Podfading" can happen for a variety of reasons, such as the creators losing interest, running out of time, or facing technical difficulties.

RSS. A type of web feed that allows apps to access updates to online content in a standardized, computer-readable format. Stands for "Really Simple Syndication".

Show notes or **shownotes**. A written summary of what was talked about in an episode, along with links to any relevant resources. This can be used as a synonym for "episode description", but typically show notes are more extensive, including external links, whereas the episode description is purely that.

Soundproofing. Making changes in your surroundings to ensure the audio you record doesn't have any unwanted background noise.

Subscriber. A person who has subscribed to a podcast through an app or platform and receives new episodes automatically as they become available. This is an ambiguous term, as it can also mean a person who pays a fee to support a podcast and gain access to exclusive content or perks. This is why some platforms are now changing to calling unpaid subscribers "followers".

Transcription. A written version of what was said in an episode.

USB. A type of connector commonly used to connect external devices to computers. A USB microphone will connect directly to your computer.

XLR. A type of connector commonly used in professional audio equipment such as microphones, mixers, and audio interfaces. An XLR microphone will not connect directly to your computer, you will need an audio interface to sit between them.

Appendix 2: Authority Maturity Model™

Researching authority

At the urging of my business coach, Philip Morgan, I started some small-scale research that eventually became a more extensive project.

I ended up surveying over 1,000 management consultants about their marketing and authority building, as well as speaking with over fifty thought leaders and experts about their personal journeys to authority.

This research was hugely beneficial in helping me to understand the world of expert professional services, and where & how marketing fits into the mix.

There are repeating patterns in how authority is built, and I developed a framework called the Authority Maturity Model™ to categorize these different stages that experts go through to become recognized as an authority in their field.

Authority Maturity Model™ stages

Novice. Everyone starts out inexperienced, and most people follow a winding path as they gain experience, figuring out what they like doing, and finding their voice and style of work.

Generalist. After gaining sufficient experience, the novice becomes an expert. At this point they are typically an invisible expert who is very good at what they do but often unknown outside of their immediate network. They are often a generalist, applying their knowledge, experience and thinking to numerous different fields and client problems. Many experts stop here, and it's possible to be a very successful expert even without broad recognition.

Specialist. If an expert chooses to remain a generalist, it's virtually impossible to become recognized as an authority. You know the phrase "a recognized authority in his/her field" — built into that is a requirement that they actually have a specialist field. A lot of experts prefer to stay generalist as niching down is counterintuitive and unappealing, but it's a crucial stage on the road to authority.

Authority. The final step in building authority is the "recognized" part, and disseminating your thinking widely is required to achieve that recognition. Typically this is done through speaking & publishing.

Most experts I speak with are either (a) generalists who need to specialize, or (b) specialists who need to work on the publishing and speaking steps.

Applying the Authority Maturity Model™

For me the interesting bit is not the framework itself, but how you can apply it to your situation.

First, you need to figure out which stage you are at in your journey: **Novice**, **Generalist**, **Specialist** or **Authority**. Progressing through the stages requires you to take appropriate action for the stage you are at.

If you are at the **Novice** stage, your priority is to gain more broad experience. This will give you a stable base of knowledge, help you figure out what you enjoy doing, and help you to start developing your voice.

If you are at the **Generalist** stage, your next step is to niche down, to specialize in a subject area. I've created a lot of resources around this topic, including a podcast called *The Specialization Podcast*.

If you are at the **Specialist** stage, the next step is to write and speak more often. Writing will help you to develop your ideas and point of view.

Publishing and speaking will grow your audience and credibility. You can also add research into the mix here: it will provide you with insights and data that is uniquely yours, giving you plenty of material to publish.

If you're already an **Authority**, you probably don't need my help. At this stage I recommend doubling down on your research, publishing and speaking efforts — including podcasting!

Visit the online resources for this book at rec.nz/resources for more about the Authority Maturity Model™.

Acknowledgements

Ugh. I hate writing this section, because of all the technical details needed elsewhere in the book, this part is the one I'm most worried about screwing up — I have a lot of people to thank, and don't want to leave anyone out by accident!

Firstly, a huge thank you to Rochelle Moulton for writing a wonderful foreword.

Rochelle and I have only spoken twice, both times on my podcast, so it was a very big ask for her to write a foreword, and I truly appreciate the wonderful job she did in introducing me and the book to the reader. Due to the power of podcasting and the "parasocial relationship", I feel like I know Rochelle very well. I've listened to countless episodes of her podcast with Jonathan Stark, The Business of Authority. I knew that I wanted Rochelle to write the foreword for this book as she gets the value of podcasting for authority. Thank you, Rochelle.

I mention the value of relationships a lot in this book. Many of those relationships started when I hired people as a coach to help me with my business. I wholeheartedly believe in the power of working with great coaches to help me on my business journey.

Philip Morgan gets several mentions in this book. That's because he has been instrumental in my business journey, helping me reinvent myself and my business. Philip is the OG "specialization" guy, a podcaster and a fantastic human being. Thank you for all your help over the past five years, Philip.

Brad Farris is another person who I've worked closely with on my business. I like Brad a lot because he likes laughing just as much as I do. Business can be fun too. Scratch that. Business SHOULD be fun too. But it's not all about the fun: Brad is a super-smart guy and great to have on your team.

Jonathan Stark is Rochelle's podcasting buddy, and is a business and podcasting coach and pricing consultant. He's also a fellow nerd, coming from the world of software development like me. When I planned to launch my first podcast, Jonathan was the first person I reached out to about it, and he sanity checked my strategy. He was also the first guest I had on the show, and helped me bring on some of the other early guests.

Adam Schaeuble is another podcasting coach I've worked with, this time on podcast audience growth. He's also been a guest on the podcast talking about just that topic. Adam is another person who likes to have a bit of fun while working, my kind of people.

I spoke with Rob Fitzpatrick on my podcast in an episode called "*How to Write Useful Books*", and subsequently joined his author coaching group, which led to a new group of friends. I hope that I've implemented Rob's advice sufficiently and you think this is a useful book! One major take-away from speaking with him that first time was the importance of beta readers to a book. I took that on board, Rob.

I owe a huge debt of gratitude to all those who agreed to beta-read this book: Aisling Snedker, Alistair McBride, Bennett Garner, Gill Moakes, Guillaume Wiatr, Joe Casabona, Jonathan Stark, Judson Rollins, Luca Ingianni, Rene Morozowich, Rie Sheridan Rose, Rory Raftery, Ross O'Boyle, Samuel Ng, Tom Nielsen, Waldemir Queiroz. All of you contributed your time in reading this book and giving me your feedback - thank you!

I particularly want to single out Alistair, Judson and Rene, whose feedback went above and beyond, into the realm of editing. They both took the time to get on calls with me to discuss the book in-depth.

Speaking of editing, I'm very lucky to have an English teacher, and an author, as parents. They've written and edited many books between them, and so I'd like to thank Joe McDermott for the line-editing and Pauline McDermott for the developmental-editing. Their work made this book easier for you to read.

A big thanks to my publisher, Melissa Wilson, who has been enthusiastic since the first time we discussed this book as a possibility, and thanks to my fellow "33 Ways" author Anne Janzer who introduced us!

Finally, for your patience, moral support, and especially your commitment to having a "real job" so I can take risks, thank you Anne-Marie!

About the author

Alastair McDermott helps "best-kept secret" experts & consultants to rapidly build authority by leveraging the power of podcasting so that you can command premium fees, cherry-pick the best projects, stop charging by-the-hour, and never have to suffer a bad-fit client again!

He is an author, consultant and business coach who hosts *The Recognized Authority Podcast*, *The Specialization Podcast*, and the *Accelerating Your Authority Podcast*.

He has written two other books so far: *Running a Website with WordPress* [2015], and *How to Sound & Look Good on Zoom & Podcasts* [2022] – published by Oak Tree Press.

Alastair lives on the beautiful west coast of Ireland. He is addicted to sports of all kinds, and he reads more science fiction and fantasy than most would consider healthy.

You can find him online at **TheRecognizedAuthority.com**

More 33 Ways

This book is part of the 33 Ways Not to Screw Up series of short, actionable business books from Networlding Publishing.

Check out the other books in the series:

- "33 Ways Not to Screw Up Consulting"
- "33 Ways Not to Screw Up Your Business Emails"
- "33 Ways Not to Screw Up Your Financial Life"
- "33 Ways Not to Screw Up Creative Entrepreneurship"
- "33 Ways Not to Screw Up Journalism"
- "33 Ways Not to Screw Up Negotiations"
- "33 Ways Not to Screw Up HR"
- "33 Ways Not to Screw Up Hiring Great Talent"

- "33 Ways Not to Screw Up Your Business Podcast"
- "33 Ways Not to Screw Up a Book Series"

You can find an up-to-date list of the 33 Ways books at **33WaysSeries.com**

Made in the USA
Columbia, SC
13 March 2023

13607623R00122